At the Table in Emilia-Ro

AT THE TABLE IN EMILIA-ROMAGNA

Author: Peter Poe

At the Table in Emilia-Romagna

Copyright © 2024 Peter Poe. All rights reserved.

At the Table in Emilia-Romagna

Summary

PREFACE 6

THE ROOTS OF EMILIAN CUISINE 9

    The Story Behind the Flavors: A Journey Through Time 10

    Artisans of Taste: Cheeses, Cured Meats, and More 16

    Innovation and Tradition in Elite Restaurants 18

    Typical Products: A Heritage to Savor 21

PROSCIUTTO PARMESAN AND BALSAMIC VINEGARD: STORIES OF EXCELLENCE 25

    Hidden Treasures: Minor but No Less Important Products 30

    Sustainability and Km 0 in Food Production 32

THE WINES OF EMILIA-ROMAGNA: A WORLD TO EXPLORE 37

    Technical Sheet: Lambrusco wine 41

    Technical Sheet: Albana di Romagna wine 43

    Technical Sheet: Pignoletto wine 46

    Technical Sheet: Malvasia sweet wine 48

    Technical Sheet: Trebbiano di Romagna wine 50

    Technical Sheet: Gutturnio wine 52

    Technical Sheet: Cagnina di Romagna wine 54

    Technical Sheet: Bianco di Custoza 57

    Technical Sheet: Barbera dell'Emilia wine 59

HISTORIC WINERIES OF EMILIA-ROMAGNA 61

FESTIVAL AND FAIRS OF EMILIA-ROMAGNA 67

    The Porcino Mushroom Festival in Borgotaro 69

The Carnival of Cento 70
The Spring Festival in Modena 73
Easter in Emilia-Romagna 74
Markets in Emilia-Romagna 76
Religious Processions: 77
Other Easter Events: 77
The "May of Bologna" 78
The Tortellino Festival in Castelfranco Emilia 78
The Parma Ham Festival 79
The Palio of Ferrara 80
The grape harvest in Romagna 81
The San Luca Fair in Bologna 82
The Truffle Festival in Sant'Agata Feltria 82
Christmas Markets 83

FRESH AND LEAVENED DOUGH: THE ART OF MANUALITY 85
THE SEA AND THE HILL: GASTRONOMIC DIVERSITYCA 88
  Tortellini, Tagliatelle and Others 89
  FISH ADND SEAFOOD 92
    Romagnolo fish broth 93
    Italian Noodles baked in foil 95
    Cuttlefish with peas 98
    Sardoncini in Beccafico alla Romagnola 100
  TRUFFLES, MUSHROOM, MEAT AND GAME 102
    Tagliatelle with Black Truffle 103
    Risotto with Porcini mushrooms 105

- Stewed wild boar 107
- Pappardelle with Hare 110
- Roast Pheasant with Mushroom Sauce 111

SWEETS AND DESSERTS 114
- Sponge cake and custard 115
- Barozzi cake 117
- Traditional Sweet cake from Romagna 118
- Bustreng 120
- Spongata of Brescello 122

THE IMPORTANCE OF PRESERVING CULINARY TRADITIONS 125

PREFACE

Dear readers,

It is with great pleasure and excitement that I present to you "At the Table in Emilia-Romagna," a journey through the rich and varied culinary landscape of one of Italy's most celebrated regions. This book is more than just a collection of recipes; it is a tribute to the history, culture, and, above all, the people who have made Emilia-Romagna an essential reference point in the gastronomic world.

Emilia-Romagna, with its historic cities like Bologna, Parma, Modena, and many others, is a land where cuisine intertwines with history and art, a region where each dish tells a story of families, traditions, and a love for the land. In these pages, we will take you on a discovery of not only traditional recipes but also the stories of those who have passed these recipes down from generation to generation, with the passion and pride that only those who deeply love their land can have.

We invite you to explore the different facets of Emilia-Romagna cuisine: from classics like Parma ham and Modena's balsamic vinegar to hand-made fresh pasta, such as tortellini and tagliatelle, and wines that have made this land famous, like Lambrusco and Sangiovese. But "At the Table in Emilia-Romagna" is not just that. It is also a journey through fairs and festivals, where cuisine becomes celebration, and through taverns and restaurants, where tradition meets innovation.

This book is dedicated to all food enthusiasts, curious travelers, lovers of Italian history and culture, but most of all to those who believe that eating is much more than a mere daily act: it is an experience, a journey, a way to know and love a land through its flavors.

Through the pages of "At the Table in Emilia-Romagna," you will discover how Emilia-Romagna dishes are the result of centuries of exchanges, encounters, and cultural contaminations, where each ingredient, each cooking method, encapsulates a piece of history and culture. We invite you to sit at our imaginary table, where each chapter is a course, each story a flavor, and every recipe an invitation to travel with us in this extraordinary Italian region.

Happy reading and, above all, bon voyage into the heart of Emilia-Romagna gastronomy.

With affection and passion,

Peter Poe

At the Table in Emilia-Romagna

THE ROOTS OF EMILIAN CUISINE

In the heart of Italy, the Emilia-Romagna region stands out not only for its cultural and historical richness but also for its distinctive culinary tradition. Emilian cuisine, with its bold flavors and generous recipes, offers a taste journey that tells stories of fertile lands, cultural encounters, and a deep passion for food.

This region, traversed by the historic Via Emilia, has always been a crossroads of peoples and cultures. Etruscans, Celts, Romans, and other groups have crossed these lands, leaving their mark not only in history but also in gastronomy. Each conqueror, migrant, or trader brought with them new ingredients, cooking techniques, and influences that have enriched the Emilian table.

The heart of Emilian cuisine beats in its high-quality raw materials. The fertile soil and favorable climate support the production of some of Italy's most iconic products, such as Parmigiano Reggiano, Prosciutto di Parma, and Balsamic Vinegar of Modena.

These world-renowned products are the result of centuries of refinement and an unmatched dedication to quality.

But it's not just the quality of the ingredients that makes Emilian cuisine special. It is also the way these are used in traditional recipes, passed down through generations. From handmade fresh pasta, like tortellini and lasagna, to hearty meat dishes and rich desserts, each recipe is a dive into the history and culture of the region.

Emilian cuisine also reflects the welcoming and generous soul of its people. Meals are seen as a time for sharing and joy, an opportunity to gather around the table and celebrate life. The famous "osterie," with their warm and informal environments, are the ideal places to savor the true essence of Emilian cuisine, where ancient recipes are served with love and pride.

The roots of Emilian cuisine are deeply intertwined with the region's history, land, and culture. Each dish tells a story, each flavor is a memory, making Emilian cuisine not only a gastronomic heritage but a true cultural treasure.

The Story Behind the Flavors: A Journey Through Time

Emilia-Romagna, located in the heart of Italy, is a region that boasts a rich and complex history, directly reflected in its extraordinary cuisine. The gastronomic journey of Emilian cuisine begins with the ancient civilizations that inhabited these lands, bringing with them traditions and flavors that laid the foundations for what we now know as Emilian cuisine.

The culinary history of the region is deeply rooted in the Roman era, when Emilia was considered the granary of Italy. This period introduced the use of grains and legumes, elements that still play a fundamental role in the local diet today. The Via Emilia, the Roman road that crosses the region, was not just a communication route but also a corridor for the exchange of products and culinary ideas, uniting different gastronomic cultures.

During the Middle Ages, Emilia-Romagna became a further evolution of its cuisine. Monasteries and abbeys in the region played a crucial role in preserving agricultural techniques and producing wine, cheese, and cured meats. This period also saw the development of some of the region's most beloved recipes, such as tortellini, a symbol of Bolognese cuisine, whose origin is lost in legend and tradition.

The arrival of the Renaissance was a time of great prosperity for Emilia-Romagna, bringing with it an era of refinement in local cuisine. The court of the Este family in Ferrara and the lords of other Emilian city-states significantly influenced the cuisine, introducing exotic ingredients and new cooking techniques. It was during this period that Emilian cuisine began to stand out for its creativity and opulence, with dishes that reflected the status and wealth of the courts.

The modern era has seen Emilian cuisine evolve further, while maintaining strong historical roots. The industrial revolution and social changes brought the spread of some traditional recipes, making them accessible to a wider audience. Today, Emilian cuisine is celebrated worldwide for its quality, simplicity, and depth of flavors, a true tribute to its rich history and cultural heritage.

Emilian cuisine, therefore, is not just a collection of delicious dishes but also a living expression of the region's history. Every recipe, every ingredient, carries centuries of traditions, cultural influences, and innovations. It is a cuisine that has adapted and evolved over time, remaining faithful to its roots.

The love and respect for traditional cuisine are reflected in the passion of local chefs, the quality of ingredients used, and the care in preparing dishes. Emilian cuisine is a true cultural experience, a journey through time that continues to enchant and satisfy palates around the world.

The story of Emilian cuisine is a fascinating narrative of evolution and tradition, a journey through time that spans centuries of history. From an ancient past to the present day, Emilian cuisine remains a fundamental pillar of the region's cultural identity, a living testament to its rich historical and culinary heritage.

At the Table in Emilia-Romagna

THE GREAT NAMES OF EMILIA-ROMAGNA CUISINE

Emilia-Romagna cuisine, renowned for its richness and variety, can also boast a series of historical and contemporary figures who have helped define and elevate its prestige. These personalities, through their talent, passion, and innovation, have left an indelible mark on the culinary tradition of this Italian region.

One of the most emblematic names associated with Emilia-Romagna cuisine is undoubtedly Pellegrino Artusi. Although he was not native to the region, his famous book "Science in the Kitchen and the Art of Eating Well" has had a significant impact on Italian cuisine in general, including many recipes from the Emilia-Romagna tradition. Artusi, with his systematic approach and passion for regional cuisine, helped codify and disseminate Emilian recipes, making them part of the national heritage.

During the 20th century, other chefs and gastronomes have contributed to promoting Emilia-Romagna cuisine. Bruno Barbieri, for example, a Michelin-starred chef, is known for his ability to reinterpret traditional dishes of the region in a modern key, while maintaining a deep respect for the ingredients and classic techniques.

Another prominent figure is Massimo Bottura, a world-famous chef whose restaurant, Osteria Francescana in Modena, has been repeatedly named among the best in the world. Bottura is celebrated for his creative and innovative approach, which, while deeply rooted in Emilia-Romagna tradition, pushes the boundaries of modern cuisine, reinterpreting classics in a bold and original way.

Equally important are those figures who, although not internationally famous, have played a crucial role in preserving and transmitting traditional recipes and techniques. Many local cooks, owners of trattorias and osterias, have dedicated their lives to guarding and celebrating the cuisine of their land, offering visitors an authentic and deeply rooted experience in Emilia-Romagna culture.

Emilian-Romagnola cuisine owes its fame and success not only to the quality of its ingredients and the richness of its traditions but also to the personalities who, over the years, have been able to interpret, innovate, and promote these dishes. These great names have helped make Emilia-Romagna cuisine a benchmark in the global gastronomic panorama, skillfully blending tradition and innovation, and ensuring that the culinary heritage of this region continues to live and evolve. Through their work, Emilian-

Romagnola cuisine is not just a pleasure for the palate but becomes a true journey into the culture and history of one of Italy's most fascinating regions.

Artisans of Taste: Cheeses, Cured Meats, and More

In the heart of Emilia-Romagna cuisine, the artisans of taste play a fundamental role in preserving and promoting the gastronomic traditions of this land. Among the fertile hills and generous plains of Emilia-Romagna, culinary treasures are hidden, resulting from centuries of artisanal knowledge: cheeses, cured meats, and many other products that are symbols of excellence worldwide.

Parmigiano Reggiano and Grana Padano are perhaps the most famous cheeses of the region, known and appreciated for their unique flavor and unmistakable colors. These cheeses, symbols of Italian craftsmanship, are the result of a production process passed down through generations, where the quality of the milk, careful processing, and long aging play an essential role. Each wheel of Parmigiano Reggiano is a small work of art, requiring patience, care, and a deep understanding of traditional methods.

The world of cured meats is rich and varied. Prosciutto di Parma and Culatello di Zibello are excellent examples of how tradition and terroir can influence the flavor and quality of a product. These cured meats, with their soft texture and rich, delicate taste, tell the story of a territory and a tradition that has been refined over time. Behind every slice of prosciutto or culatello, there is the meticulous work of artisans who select the best meats and follow ancient processes for salting and aging.

Beyond the famous cheeses and cured meats, Emilia-Romagna offers a wide range of other artisanal products. From vinegar producers of Traditional Balsamic Vinegar of Modena to small companies that make preserves, sauces, and pestos following ancient recipes, each product is an expression of the territory and its culture.

The artisans of taste in Emilia-Romagna are not only guardians of age-old techniques and traditions; they are also innovators who experiment with new ideas while remaining faithful to quality and authenticity. This balance between innovation and tradition is the key to the success of Emilia-Romagna products, which continue to win appreciation worldwide.

The dedication of the artisans of taste extends beyond production: many are also engaged in disseminating the gastronomic culture of the region, offering tastings, guided tours of their companies, and workshops. These experiences allow visitors to immerse themselves in the history and culture of the region, understand the production process, and fully appreciate the work and passion behind each product.

The artisans of taste from Emilia-Romagna are true ambassadors of the region's gastronomic culture. Through their work, they keep traditions alive, promote the excellence of local products, and contribute to spreading the prestige of Emilia-Romagna cuisine worldwide. Their commitment and passion are fundamental in preserving the culinary heritage of this land, making it accessible and appreciated by an increasingly broad and international audience.

Innovation and Tradition in Elite Restaurants

In Emilia-Romagna cuisine, innovation and tradition blend harmoniously, especially in the elite restaurants that dot the region. These culinary temples are not merely places to eat; they are platforms where culinary history meets contemporary creativity, creating a gastronomic experience that transcends time and place.

Elite restaurants in Emilia-Romagna have earned a prominent place on the global gastronomic map. Internationally renowned chefs like Massimo Bottura, with his celebrated Osteria Francescana in Modena, have redefined regional cuisine, elevating it to new heights of recognition and appreciation. In these venues, traditional dishes are reinvented, respecting local ingredients and ancestral techniques, yet presented in a modern and innovative way.

These restaurants are idea labs where tradition is not seen as a constraint, but as a solid foundation from which to explore new possibilities. Simple ingredients from Emilia-Romagna home cooking are transformed into sophisticated dishes that surprise the palate and challenge expectations. The goal is twofold: to honor the roots of regional cuisine while pushing the boundaries of contemporary gastronomy.

Experimentation in these elite restaurants goes beyond food. It extends to the environment itself, the service, and the overall customer experience. Many of these restaurants combine innovative design with welcoming atmospheres, creating a context in which every meal becomes a memorable event. The service is also an integral part of the experience, with staff who not only serve food but narrate the story of each dish, connecting the diner's present with the region's history.

These restaurants also play a significant role in the local economy. They support small producers and artisans of taste by selecting high-quality ingredients produced in the region. This not only ensures an authentic gastronomic experience for customers but also helps preserve and promote the agricultural and culinary heritage of Emilia-Romagna.

The elite restaurants of Emilia-Romagna are much more than places where one can savor excellent dishes. They are custodians of a rich culinary tradition and at the same time, pioneers of a new gastronomic era. Through their relentless pursuit of excellence, they manage to celebrate the past while simultaneously writing the future of Emilia-Romagna cuisine, making it one of the most exciting and dynamic in the global culinary landscape.

With their commitment to merging the old with the new, these restaurants not only offer unforgettable culinary experiences but also continue to position Emilia-Romagna as an essential destination for gastronomy enthusiasts from around the world.

This synergy between innovation and tradition is a shining example of how cuisine can be a powerful means to celebrate culture, experiment with new ideas, and share unique stories, making every dish an exciting journey through history and taste.

In Emilia-Romagna, there are several elite restaurants that have gained fame both nationally and internationally. Here are some examples of renowned restaurants in the Romagna region and their locations:

Osteria Francescana - Located in Modena, this restaurant is led by chef Massimo Bottura, a prominent figure in contemporary Italian cuisine. The Restaurant is famous for its innovative cuisine that remains deeply rooted in Emilia-Romagna tradition.

Antica Osteria del Mirasole - This restaurant is located in San Giovanni in Persiceto, near Bologna. It is known for its authentic and traditional approach to Romagna cuisine, with a particular focus on local and seasonal products.

Da Gorini - Located in San Piero in Bagno, a small village in the province of Forlì-Cesena, this restaurant is known for its creative cuisine that combines modern techniques with traditional Romagna flavors.

La Frasca - This restaurant is situated in Cervia, known for its cuisine that reflects the richness of the Romagna territory, with a particular emphasis on fresh seafood and local ingredients.

Il Ristorante Marconi - In Sasso Marconi, near Bologna, this restaurant is renowned for its innovative cuisine that experiments with traditional ingredients and techniques, offering a unique culinary experience.

San Domenico - Located in Imola, this historic restaurant is a true institution in Italian cuisine. Known for its excellent food and rich wine cellar, San Domenico offers a perfect fusion of tradition and innovation.

Al Caminetto - In Torriana, near Rimini, this restaurant offers a cuisine that combines tradition and creativity, with a particular focus on local and seasonal products.

Each of these restaurants represents a unique aspect of Romagna cuisine, offering their guests a culinary experience that goes beyond the simple act of eating, becoming a journey into the culture and tradition of the region.

Typical Products: A Heritage to Savor

Emilia-Romagna is a region distinguished not only by its rich history and culture but also by the abundance and quality of its typical products. These products, ranging from cheeses to cured meats, from wines to condiments, are more than just ingredients; they are a heritage to savor, a tangible expression of the land and tradition of this rich Italian region.

Cheeses are a pride of Emilia-Romagna, with Parmigiano Reggiano leading the way. This cheese, known worldwide for its intense flavor and versatility, is the result of an artisanal production process handed down through generations. Each wheel of Parmigiano Reggiano is a concentration of ancient knowledge and passion for quality, representing one of the symbols of Italian gastronomic excellence.

Cured meats are another feather in the cap of the region. Prosciutto di Parma, with its delicate taste and soft color, is the result of a meticulous aging process and a tradition that goes back centuries. Similarly, Culatello di Zibello and Mortadella di Bologna are examples of how the art of charcuterie in Emilia-Romagna is a form of cultural expression, as well as an economic activity.

One cannot discuss the typical products of Emilia-Romagna without mentioning Balsamic Vinegar of Modena. This condiment, with its unique and complex flavor, is the fruit of a long and laborious aging process in a series of different wooden barrels. Each drop of Balsamic Vinegar encapsulates the history and taste of a land that has made quality and excellence its fundamental principles.

The wines of the region, such as Lambrusco and Sangiovese, are equally representative. These wines, with their distinctive character, perfectly complement the richness of the Emilian-Romagna dishes, completing the region's gastronomic experience.

These typical products are not just ingredients for traditional Emilia-Romagna dishes; they are symbols of a cultural heritage expressed through food. The production of these products is steeped in history, passion, and a deep connection to the territory. They are the result of a balance between innovation and respect for traditions, a balance that ensures the continuity and quality of these gastronomic excellences.

The typical products of Emilia-Romagna are true gastronomic treasures that tell stories of fertile lands, artisanal knowledge, and a culture that venerates good food. These products are not only appreciated locally but also serve as ambassadors of the region around the world, carrying with them the taste, aroma, and spirit of one of Italy's richest and most vibrant regions.

Tasting these products means embarking on a sensory journey that spans centuries of tradition and innovation, a journey that renews appreciation for the simplicity and purity of authentic flavors. In every bite of these typical products, one can sense the commitment, passion, and pride of a region that has made its cuisine an art to share and celebrate.

At the Table in Emilia-Romagna

PROSCIUTTO PARMESAN AND BALSAMIC VINEGARD: STORIES OF EXCELLENCE

The heart of Emilia-Romagna cuisine is populated by a trilogy of products that have become globally synonymous with gastronomic excellence: Prosciutto di Parma, Parmigiano Reggiano and Aceto Balsamico di Modena. These products are not only fundamental ingredients in Italian cuisine; they are also representative of a profound history, an artisanal tradition and a cultural identity that defines Emilia-Romagna.

Prosciutto di Parma: A Masterpiece of Flavour is known and celebrated all over the world for its delicate taste and soft texture, representing one of the highest expressions of the Italian culinary tradition.

This product, born from an ancient tradition and knowledge handed down through generations, is today one of the most prestigious ambassadors of Italian cuisine abroad.

The production of Prosciutto di Parma follows a rigorous, centuries-old process that begins with the careful selection of meat and continues with balanced salting and curing for up to 24 months. This traditional method not only guarantees the ham's exceptional quality, but is also a tribute to the cultural and historical roots of the Emilia-Romagna region.

In recent years, Parma Ham has seen exponential growth in its exports, becoming a product in demand in many international markets. The United States is the largest foreign market for Parma Ham, where it is highly valued for its unique flavour and versatility in cooking. Other significant markets include European countries such as France, Germany and the United Kingdom, where demand for authentic, high quality products continues to grow.

In Asia, countries such as Japan, China and South Korea have shown increasing interest in Parma Ham. In these nations, ham is often considered a luxury product, valued both for its flavour and for its symbolic status. The growing interest in Western cuisine and high-quality food products has opened up new market opportunities in these regions.

The global expansion of Parma Ham has not only contributed significantly to the economy of Emilia-Romagna and Italy as a whole but has also played a key role in promoting Italian culture and taste abroad. The success of Parma Ham in international markets is a testament to its unparalleled quality and its ability to adapt to the tastes and preferences of different cultures, while maintaining its indissoluble link with the tradition and history of its region of origin.

Parmigiano Reggiano: recognised as one of the finest cheeses in the world, it is a true symbol of the art of Italian cheesemaking. Its production, which is based on traditional methods and a rigorous selection of ingredients, has made it an internationally renowned product and a pillar of Italy's agricultural and food exports.

This cheese, known for its complexity of flavours and crystalline texture, is the result of a meticulous artisanal process. The milk used for Parmigiano Reggiano comes exclusively from cows reared in the defined geographical area of Emilia-Romagna, and its long ripening period, which can exceed 36 months, contributes to its unmistakable taste and unique texture.

Parmigiano Reggiano's popularity has transcended Italian borders, making it one of the most exported and loved cheeses abroad. Europe remains one of the main markets for Parmigiano Reggiano exports, with high demand in countries such as France, Germany and the United Kingdom. However, recent years have also seen a significant growth in its popularity outside Europe, particularly in the United States, Canada and Asia.

In the US, Parmigiano Reggiano is highly valued for its versatility and is used in a wide range of recipes, from home cooking to gourmet restaurant menus.

In Asia, countries such as China and Japan are showing a growing interest in high quality Italian cheeses, and Parmigiano

Reggiano, with its distinctive flavour and rich history, is establishing itself as a prestigious product in these emerging markets.

The importance of Parmigiano Reggiano in Italian exports is not limited to its economic value. The cheese is also an ambassador of Italian culture and taste, representing the tradition, quality and excellence that characterise 'made in Italy'. The growing international demand for Parmigiano Reggiano testifies to the global recognition of its superior quality and appreciation for traditional Italian craftsmanship.

In conclusion, Parmigiano Reggiano is not only a key ingredient in many Italian recipes; it is an icon of Italian gastronomy and a key player in the world of food exports. Its worldwide fame and growing demand in international markets underline its role as one of the greatest ambassadors of Italian taste and quality in the world.

Traditional Balsamic Vinegar of Modena: with its distinctive flavour and rich history, it has become one of the most famous and sought-after condiments globally. This emblematic product of Emilia-Romagna is the result of a meticulous ageing process and an artisanal tradition dating back centuries.

The process of making Balsamic Vinegar of Modena is an art that requires time, dedication and great expertise. Aged in series of barrels made from different types of wood, this vinegar gradually develops a perfect balance of sweetness and acidity, as well as a wide range of aromas and flavours that make it unique. The length and complexity of this process not only give the vinegar its distinctive characteristics, but are also a symbol of the value of patience and respect for ancient traditions.

The fame of Balsamic Vinegar of Modena has long transcended Italian borders, making it a product of great demand on international markets. In the United States and Canada, it is particularly appreciated for its versatility and is used both in cooking and as an ingredient in innovative gastronomic creations. In Europe, it is an indispensable condiment in the kitchens of many countries, loved for its ability to enrich a wide range of dishes.

In Asia, Balsamic Vinegar of Modena is gaining popularity, especially among consumers looking for unique, high-quality products. In markets such as China and Japan, it is often perceived as a luxury product and is used in sophisticated dishes and haute cuisine restaurants.

The importance of Balsamic Vinegar of Modena in Italian exports is not limited to its economic value. This product is a bearer of Italian history and food and wine culture, representing the excellence and creativity that characterize Italian cuisine. Its growing popularity in foreign markets reflects a growing worldwide interest in authentic, quality products, and testifies to Italy's ability to create gastronomic products that are appreciated and desired all over the world.

Balsamic Vinegar of Modena is not only a condiment with a rich and complex taste; it is also a symbol of Italian tradition, quality and excellence that continues to conquer palates and markets around the world.

Prosciutto di Parma, Parmigiano Reggiano and Balsamic Vinegar of Modena are not only prominent products in the cuisine of Emilia-Romagna; they are emblems of a food and wine culture that values quality, tradition and craftsmanship. These products represent stories of excellence, where centuries of knowledge, dedication and passion come together to create flavours that are celebrated all over the world.

Their production is not just a culinary process; it is a ritual, a celebration of the land and its people. To taste these products is to immerse oneself in a journey through the history and culture of a region that has made food an art form. Through their taste, these products tell the story of a rich and generous land, and a population that has been able to transform nature's gifts into gastronomic masterpieces.

Hidden Treasures: Minor but No Less Important Products

In the shadows of Emilia-Romagna's best-known excellences, such as Prosciutto di Parma, Parmigiano Reggiano and Balsamic Vinegar, are hidden treasures: minor products that, although less famous, are just as important in defining the region's rich gastronomic landscape. These products, often overlooked by the international spotlight, are indispensable to fully understand the diversity and depth of Emilia-Romagna cuisine.

One of these treasures is Culatello di Zibello, a prized cured meat produced in a restricted area near the Po river. Less well known than its 'cousin' Prosciutto di Parma, Culatello is just as sought after by connoisseurs for its intense flavour and delicate texture, the result of a long and careful maturing process in the ancient damp cellars of the Bassa Parmense.

Another hidden gem is Spongata, a traditional sweet prepared mainly during the Christmas season. Originating in Busseto, this cake is a kind of pie filled with jam, candied fruit, dried fruit and spices. Every family has its own recipe, jealously guarded and handed down from generation to generation.

One cannot talk about the hidden treasures of Emilia-Romagna without mentioning its lesser-known but no less valuable wines. In addition to the famous Lambrusco and Sangiovese, the region produces excellent white wines such as Pignoletto and Malvasia, which are slowly gaining recognition both nationally and internationally for their freshness and versatility.

Even in the field of cheeses, in addition to the famous Parmigiano Reggiano, there are lesser known gems such as Squacquerone, a soft and creamy cheese typical of Romagna, perfect for spreading on piadina. And then there is Caciotta, a soft cheese produced in different varieties, ranging from fresh to seasoned with herbs or spices.

These products, although they may be considered 'minor' compared to the giants of regional gastronomy, are fundamental to understanding the true essence of Emilia-Romagna cuisine. Each product encapsulates a history, a territory and a tradition. They are the result of a deep connection with the land and the agricultural and artisanal practices that define the region.

Moreover, these products play a crucial role in the local economy, supporting small farms, artisan producers and rural communities. Their production and marketing help to keep local traditions alive and promote a sustainable, land-based lifestyle.

The rediscovery and valorisation of these hidden treasures is becoming increasingly important in the context of modern food and wine. As consumers become increasingly interested in the origin of products and the history behind the food they eat, the minor products of Emilia-Romagna offer rich and authentic stories.

Local restaurants, wine bars and farmers' markets are beginning to highlight these products, offering visitors the opportunity to explore a wider range of flavours and traditions. This not only helps preserve the gastronomic diversity of the region, but also offers visitors a richer and deeper culinary experience.

The minor products of Emilia-Romagna are hidden treasures that deserve to be discovered and celebrated. They represent a fundamental aspect of the region's gastronomic culture, enriching the food and wine scene with their uniqueness and authenticity. These products, with their stories, flavours and traditions, are a living testimony of Emilia-Romagna's cultural heritage and an invitation to explore the depth and variety of one of Italy's richest regional cuisines.

Sustainability and Km 0 in Food Production

In food production in Emilia-Romagna, two concepts are becoming increasingly important: sustainability and the concept of

'Km 0'. These principles, applied in the production of delicacies such as Prosciutto di Parma, Parmigiano Reggiano and Balsamic Vinegar of Modena, are helping to redefine the way these traditional products are made, placing a new emphasis on the environment, quality and health.

Sustainability in food production implies rigorous attention to the environmental impact of each stage of the production process. In the case of Parma Ham, this means adopting practices that reduce the carbon footprint, from meat selection to pig breeding to curing. Conscious producers are implementing strategies to reduce energy consumption and use renewable energy sources, as well as promoting sustainable animal husbandry and welfare.

In the case of Parmigiano Reggiano, sustainability translates into a controlled supply chain, where milk comes exclusively from local farms, guaranteeing not only freshness and quality, but also reducing transport and thus greenhouse gas emissions. Many dairies are adopting more ecological production methods, such as the use of solar energy or biogas produced from agricultural waste to minimise environmental impact.

Balsamic Vinegar of Modena, for its part, benefits from sustainable farming practices in the cultivation of grapes, with increased interest in organic farming and reduced use of pesticides and chemical fertilisers. The production of this vinegar often involves small local vinegar producers, who maintain centuries-old traditions while respecting the environment and the local community.

The concept of 'Km 0', or short supply chain, is another key aspect of this new wave of sustainability. It involves favouring the use of locally produced ingredients, reducing the kilometres travelled by food before it reaches the consumer. This

approach not only guarantees the freshness and authenticity of products, but also supports the local economy and significantly reduces the environmental impact of long-distance transport.

In the case of Prosciutto di Parma, Parmigiano Reggiano and Balsamic Vinegar of Modena, the adoption of the Km 0 principle means that most of the production processes, from raw material to processing, take place within the Emilia-Romagna region. This not only strengthens the link between the products and their territory of origin, but also ensures that agricultural and production practices meet the highest standards in terms of quality and sustainability.

A commitment to sustainability and zero food miles also has a positive impact on consumer health. Products made with fresh, local ingredients, without the excessive use of preservatives or chemical additives, offer superior nutritional quality and contribute to a healthier, more balanced diet.

In addition, these sustainable practices and the zero-mile philosophy are strengthening the link between consumers and the land, increasing awareness about the origin of food and local culinary traditions. This is leading to a greater appreciation of typical products and a renewed interest in the recipes and traditional food habits of the Emilia-Romagna region.

In conclusion, the approach to sustainability and Km 0 in the production of some of Emilia-Romagna's most iconic products represents a significant change in the food sector. This change not only responds to the growing demands of an increasingly environmentally and health-conscious market, but also helps to preserve and enhance the gastronomic traditions of one of Italy's richest and most diverse regions.

Through these practices, Prosciutto di Parma, Parmigiano Reggiano and Aceto Balsamico di Modena are not only expressions of culinary excellence, but also become symbols of a more sustainable and conscious future in the world of food. In this way, these products not only maintain their worldwide prestige and reputation, but also evolve to meet the challenges of our time, showing how tradition can go hand in hand with innovation and respect for the environment.

THE WINES OF EMILIA-ROMAGNA: A WORLD TO EXPLORE

Emilia-Romagna, a region famous for its gastronomic products such as Prosciutto di Parma, Parmigiano Reggiano, and Balsamic Vinegar, is also a land of extraordinary and diverse wines. These wines, although less known compared to other regional excellences, constitute a fascinating and rich world of discovery for wine enthusiasts.

Thanks to its geographic diversity ranging from hills to plains, the Emilia-Romagna territory offers ideal conditions for viticulture. This variety of landscapes is reflected in a surprising range of wines, each with its unique characteristics, closely tied to its terroir of origin.

One of the most representative wines of the region is Lambrusco. This sparkling wine, often associated with pleasant freshness and fruity notes, is perfect paired with the rich flavors of the region's cured meats and cheeses. With several varieties coming from specific sub-zones, Lambrusco can range from dry to sweetly fruity, displaying a surprising complexity that dispels the myth of it being merely a light and summery wineAnother oenological gem of Emilia-Romagna is Sangiovese di Romagna.

This red wine, made from the Sangiovese grape, is known for its robustness and depth, with notes of ripe fruit and spices, accompanied by a well-balanced tannic structure. Perfect paired with meat dishes and game, Sangiovese di Romagna is an excellent example of how a wine can express the character of a territory.

In addition to these two pillars, the region also produces a variety of white wines, like Pignoletto, which is gaining popularity for its fresh aromatic profile and liveliness. Native to the Bolognese hills, Pignoletto is notable for its floral and fruity hints, with a slight effervescence that makes it particularly enjoyable and refreshing. It is an ideal wine to accompany light appetizers, fish dishes, and fresh cheeses.

Furthermore, Emilia-Romagna also offers excellent examples of dessert and passito wines, like Albana di Romagna Passito. This wine, made from dried Albana grapes, has a richness and complexity of flavors ranging from candied fruit to honey and spices. It is a wine that surprises with its structure and intensity, perfect to enjoy with desserts or as an after-dinner meditation.

The exploration of Emilia-Romagna's wines is not complete without mentioning its sparkling wines. Produced using the classical or charmat method, the Emilian-Romagnolo sparkling wine stands out for its finesse and elegance, offering a refined choice for celebrating special occasions or for toasts that emphasize taste and quality.

The variety and quality of Emilian-Romagnolo wines are the result of a unique mix of tradition, terroir, and innovation. The region's winemakers, with a deep understanding of their land and a constant commitment to quality, continue to explore and experiment, elevating the wines of Emilia-Romagna to new levels of excellence.

In conclusion, the wines of Emilia-Romagna represent a rich and varied oenological world, ready to be explored by wine lovers. These wines are not only the perfect complement to the region's famous gastronomy but are also authentic expressions of a territory that has much to offer.

Every glass of Emilian-Romagnolo wine encapsulates a story of passion, dedication, and territorial identity, inviting on a sensory journey that enhances the flavors and traditions of one of Italy's most gastronomically rich regions. Discovering these wines is a fascinating adventure, a journey that leads through enchanting landscapes, stories of passionate producers, and flavors that linger in the memory.

Ultimately, the wines of the Emilia-Romagna land are a heritage to be preserved, celebrated, and above all, savored. Emilia-Romagna, an Italian region known for its rich gastronomic tradition, produces a variety of wines that reflect the diversity of its territory. Here is a list of the most representative wines of the region:

"Lambrusco" wine: Perhaps the most famous wine of Emilia-Romagna, Lambrusco is a light and fruity red or rosé sparkling wine, perfect for pairing with the typical dishes of the regional cuisine.

"Sangiovese di Romagna" wine: A robust and structured red wine, Sangiovese di Romagna is known for its aromas of ripe red fruits and a slight spicy note.

"Pignoletto" wine: A sparkling or still white wine, Pignoletto has a fresh and lively aromatic profile, with hints of flowers and fruit.

"Albana di Romagna" wine: The first Italian white wine to receive the DOCG designation, Albana can be dry, semi-sweet, or sweet (passito), and is known for its richness and complexity.

"Malvasia" wine: Produced mainly in the Parma area, this variety yields aromatic wines, both sparkling and still, with floral and ripe fruit notes.

"Trebbiano di Romagna" wine: A light and fresh white wine, often with a touch of lively acidity, making it a great pairing for fish dishes and seafood.

"Gutturnio" wine: Produced mainly in the province of Piacenza, it is a blend of Barbera and Bonarda, which can be still or sparkling, characterized by red fruit notes and a pleasant freshness.

"Colli di Parma Rosso" wine: A typical red wine of the Colli Parma area, often a blend of various varieties, offering a range of medium to full-bodied flavors.

"Colli di Parma Bianco" wine: A white wine from the hilly areas of Parma, which can be produced from different grape varieties, offering a fresh and slightly fruity taste.

"Cagnina di Romagna" wine: A sweet, light, and fruity red wine, typically produced in Romagna, that pairs well with sweets and desserts.

"Bianco di Custoza" wine: Although more associated with the Veneto region, some areas of Emilia-Romagna produce this white wine, known for its freshness and floral notes.

"Barbera dell'Emilia" wine: A lively and fruity red wine, with good acidity, making this wine versatile and suitable for various culinary pairings.

"Bonarda dell'Emilia" wine: Usually sparkling, this red wine is known for its red fruit flavors and a slight sweetness.

Each wine from this region expresses the uniqueness of its territory and wine traditions, offering a range of flavors and styles that can satisfy a wide variety of palates. From the sparkling Lambrusco to the robust Sangiovese, from aromatic whites to structured reds, Emilia-Romagna has much to offer wine enthusiasts.

Technical Sheet: Lambrusco wine

Origin and Designation: Lambrusco is a sparkling wine native to Emilia-Romagna, Italy. It is produced in various sub-zones of the region, each with its own specific Denomination of Origin (DOC).

- Grape Varieties: Lambrusco is primarily made from the grape variety of the same name, which includes several strains such as Lambrusco Salamino, Lambrusco Grasparossa, Lambrusco di Sorbara, among others.

Organoleptic Characteristics:

- Color: Ruby red, often with violet hues. Some varieties may be lighter.
- Aroma: Fruity and floral aroma, with notes of strawberry, cherry, and sometimes violets.
- Taste: Fresh and fruity flavor, with pleasant acidity and characteristic effervescence. Sweetness varies from dry to sweet, depending on the style.
- Alcohol Content: Usually ranges from 10.5% to 12.5% by volume.
- Production Method: Lambrusco is often produced using the Charmat method, where the second fermentation occurs in large closed pressure vessels to maintain natural effervescence.
- Styles: Lambrusco can be found in various styles, from sparkling to still, and from dry to sweetly fruity.

Food Pairings:

- Cured Meats and Cold Cuts: Pairs beautifully with Prosciutto di Parma, salami, and other charcuterie specialties thanks to its acidity and fizz, which balance the fat and rich flavor of the meats.

- Pasta Dishes: Excellent with traditional pasta dishes, particularly those with meat-based sauces, such as lasagna or tortellini in broth.
- Cheeses: Pairs well with a variety of cheeses, especially fresh or semi-aged ones. The acidity and bubbles of Lambrusco cut through the richness of the cheese.
- Grilled Meats and Roasts: Ideal with grilled red meats, barbecue, and roasts, where its freshness pleasantly contrasts with the richness of the meat.
- Vegetarian Cuisine: A good match for vegetarian dishes, especially those with grilled vegetables or rich salads.
- Pizza: Perfect with pizza, particularly those with rich and flavorful toppings such as salami or prosciutto.
- Sweets and Desserts: Sweeter versions of Lambrusco can be paired with desserts, especially those based on fruit or less sugary baked goods.

In general, Lambrusco, with its variety of styles, offers a flexible range of food pairings, making it an ideal wine for multiple occasions and dishes.

Technical Sheet: Albana di Romagna wine

Origin and Designation: Albana di Romagna is an Italian white wine from the Romagna region of Emilia-Romagna. It was the first white wine in Italy to receive the Controlled and Guaranteed Denomination of Origin (DOCG) status.

Grape Variety: Produced exclusively from Albana grapes, a native variety of Romagna.

Organoleptic Characteristics:

- Color: Ranges from straw yellow to golden, depending on the style and aging.
- Aroma: Notes of ripe fruit, white flowers, and in some cases hints of honey, apricot, and spices.
- Flavor: Rich and full-bodied, with good acidity. It can vary from dry to sweet, especially in the passito versions, which feature intense and sweet flavors.
- Alcohol Content: Generally varies from 12% to 15% by volume, depending on the style.
- Production Method: Albana di Romagna can be produced in several styles, including dry, semi-sweet, sweet, and passito. The passito is made from dried grapes, which concentrate the sugar and flavors, producing a rich and complex wine.

Food Pairings:

Dry Version:

- Fish and Seafood Dishes: Classic pairings include grilled fish, seafood, and fish carpaccio.
- Fresh Cheeses: Pairs well with fresh and light cheeses.
- Vegetables and Salads: Great with vegetable-based dishes, both raw and cooked.

Semi-Sweet Version:

- Asian Dishes: Pairs well with Asian cuisine, especially dishes with a slight sweetness, like some Thai or Chinese dishes.

- Light Starters: Ideal with appetizers and vegetable-based dishes, especially if they have a slightly sweet or sweet-sour component.

Sweet and Passito Version:

- Sweets and Desserts: Perfect with fruit desserts, dry pastries, and less sugary sweets. Also excellent with tiramisu.
- Blue Cheeses: Surprisingly good with blue or spicy cheeses, creating an interesting taste contrast.
- Foie Gras: Pairs with foie gras, offering a rich and complex flavor balance.

General Pairings:

Romagna Cuisine Dishes: Albana di Romagna naturally pairs with dishes from Romagna cuisine, from fresh pasta starters to main courses of white meat and fish.

Albana di Romagna is a wine that surprises with its ability to accompany a wide range of dishes, from simple and rustic cuisine to more refined and complex dishes. Its variety of styles makes it an extremely versatile wine, adaptable to different occasions and culinary preferences. Whether in a dry, semi-sweet, or passito version, Albana di Romagna has a unique ability to enhance the flavors of the dishes it is paired with, offering a delightful discovery for wine lovers and gourmets alike. Ultimately, Albana di Romagna is not just a wine of great pleasure to drink, but also an explorer of culinary pairings, capable of opening new horizons in the world of taste and gastronomy.

Technical Sheet: Pignoletto wine

Origin and Designation: Pignoletto is a typical white wine of Emilia-Romagna, particularly from the hilly areas around Bologna. The designation includes both still (tranquilly) and sparkling versions.

- Grape Variety: Primarily made from Pignoletto grapes, a native vine of Emilia-Romagna.

Organoleptic Characteristics:

- Color: Straw yellow, sometimes with greenish reflections.
- Aroma: Fresh and delicate aroma, with floral and fruity notes, which may include green apple, citrus, white flowers, and occasionally hints of hazelnut.
- Flavor: In the mouth, Pignoletto presents good acidity, freshness, and characteristic savory notes. The flavors may echo the olfactory notes, with a pleasantly lively finish, especially in the sparkling version.
- Alcohol Content: Generally between 11% and 13%.
- Production Method: Pignoletto can be produced in both still and sparkling versions. The sparkling version is often made using the Charmat method (tank fermentation), which gives the wine its typical effervescence.

Food Pairings:

With its freshness and savoriness, Pignoletto is extremely versatile in terms of food pairings:

- Light Starters: Perfect with fish-based appetizers, carpaccio, seafood, and light cured meats.
- Fish and Seafood Dishes: Pairs well with a wide range of fish dishes, both raw and cooked, including sushi and sashimi.
- Vegetarian Cuisine: The acidity and freshness of Pignoletto make it an excellent complement to vegetarian dishes, such as fresh salads, grilled vegetables, or legume-based dishes.
- Fresh Cheeses: Matches well with fresh and medium-aged cheeses, such as ricotta, goat cheese, or Squacquerone.
- Regional Cuisine Dishes: Ideal with typical Emilian-Romagnola dishes, such as tortellini in broth, green lasagna, or stuffed piadina.
- White Meat Dishes: Its lightness makes it a good companion for lightly seasoned chicken, turkey, or pork dishes.
- Aperitif: The sparkling version of Pignoletto is perfect as an aperitif, thanks to its freshness and vivacity.

In general, Pignoletto is a wine that enhances delicate flavors and does not overpower the dishes it is paired with, making it an excellent choice for a wide variety of culinary occasions. Its versatility makes it suitable for both everyday meals and special occasions.

Technical Sheet: Malvasia sweet wine

Origin and Designation: Malvasia is a typical wine of Emilia-Romagna, with various variants produced in different areas of the region. Malvasia di Parma is one of the best known.

- Grape Variety: Produced primarily from the Malvasia grape variety, which in Emilia-Romagna can be Malvasia di Candia Aromatica or other local variants.

Organoleptic Characteristics:

- Color: Generally straw yellow, sometimes with golden hues.
- Aroma: Characterized by an intense aromatic bouquet, with floral and fruity notes that may include peach, apricot, apple, and sometimes hints of sweet spices or aromatic herbs.
- Flavor: On the palate, Malvasia ranges from dry to sweet, with good acidity that balances the sweetness. The flavors reflect the olfactory notes with a pleasant aromatic persistence.
- Alcohol Content: Generally varies between 11% and 13.5%.
- Production Method: Malvasia can be produced in various versions, from still to sparkling, and from dry to sweet. The sparkling version is often made through the Charmat method (tank fermentation), which gives the wine its characteristic effervescence, while the still version is fermented without the addition of carbon dioxide.

Food Pairings:

With its range of styles and aromatic profile, Malvasia offers various pairing possibilities with food:

Dry Version:

- Appetizers and Snacks: Pairs well with light appetizers, mildly spiced cured meats, and fresh cheeses.
- Fish and Seafood Dishes: Excellent with light fish dishes, both steamed and grilled, and with seafood.
- Vegetarian Cuisine: Interesting pairings can be created with fresh salads, grilled vegetables, and delicate vegetarian dishes.

Sparkling Version:

- Aperitif: Perfect as an aperitif drink, accompanying salty snacks or assorted tastings.
- Regional Cuisine Dishes: Pairs well with typical Emilian-Romagna dishes, such as savory pies or stuffed flatbreads.
- Ethnic Cuisine: Can be an interesting pairing with Asian cuisine, especially dishes that are not overly spicy.

Sweet Version:

- Desserts and Sweets: Ideal with fruit desserts, pastries, and less sugary desserts.
- Blue or Aged Cheeses: In particular, the sweet version of Malvasia pairs magnificently with rich and flavorful cheeses, such as Gorgonzola or other blue cheeses.

- Mediterranean Cuisine: Dry Malvasia pairs well with Mediterranean dishes that include aromatic herbs, olives, and tomato-based ingredients.
- White Meat Dishes: The freshness and aromaticity of dry Malvasia also make it suitable for dishes based on chicken or rabbit, especially if prepared with aromatic herbs or light sauces.

Malvasia from Emilia-Romagna is a wine that can offer extremely diverse culinary experiences depending on its style. Whether it is a dry, sparkling, or sweet version, Malvasia is capable of enhancing a variety of flavors and dishes, making it an excellent choice for experimenting with different culinary pairings. Its versatility makes it a highly appreciated wine for both casual occasions and more refined meals, always providing a pleasant and satisfying tasting experience.

Technical Sheet: Trebbiano di Romagna wine

Origin and Designation: Trebbiano di Romagna is a white wine from the Emilia-Romagna region in Italy, specifically from the Romagna area. It belongs to the Trebbiano family of wines, one of the most widely planted grape varieties in Italy.

Grape Variety: Primarily made from the Trebbiano Romagnolo grape variety.

Organoleptic Characteristics:

- Color: Generally light straw yellow, with possible greenish reflections.
- Aroma: Characterized by a delicate and subtle fragrance, with notes of white flowers, fresh fruit such as apple and pear, and sometimes citrus hints.
- Flavor: On the palate, it is typically fresh and light, with good acidity. The flavor follows the olfactory notes, offering a clean and refreshing taste.
- Alcohol Content: Generally varies between 11% and 12.5%.
- Production Method: The vinification of Trebbiano di Romagna follows the traditional method for white wines, with fermentation at controlled temperatures to preserve the fresh and fruity aromas of the grape.

Food Pairings:

With its freshness and lightness, Trebbiano di Romagna is an extremely versatile wine for food pairings:

- Fish Dishes: Pairs beautifully with light fish dishes, such as seafood starters, grilled or steamed fish, and seafood salads.
- Regional Cuisine: Complements typical Romagnola dishes well, such as passatelli in broth, piadina stuffed with squacquerone cheese, and other light local cuisine.
- Fresh Cheeses: Excellent with fresh and soft cheeses, such as mozzarella, stracchino, or ricotta.

- Vegetables: Matches well with vegetable-based dishes, such as mixed salads, grilled or steamed vegetables, and light appetizers.
- Asian Cuisine: Can be paired with light Asian dishes, such as sushi and sashimi, thanks to its ability to balance flavors without overpowering them.
- White Meat Dishes: Also suitable for accompanying light white meats, such as chicken or turkey, especially if prepared simply.
- Aperitif: Its freshness also makes it suitable as an aperitif wine, particularly on warm summer days.

Trebbiano's Romagna is a wine that, with its freshness and lightness, adapts to a variety of culinary contexts, making it an excellent choice for both everyday meals and special occasions.

Technical Sheet: Gutturnio wine

Origin and Designation: Gutturnio is a red wine from the province of Piacenza in Emilia-Romagna, Italy. It is a wine with a Controlled and Guaranteed Designation of Origin (DOCG) that combines two grape varieties: Barbera and Bonarda (locally known as Croatina).

Grape Varieties: The typical blend for Gutturnio includes a majority of Barbera, and Bonarda. Barbera provides structure and acidity, while Bonarda adds softness and fruity notes.

Organoleptic Characteristics:

- Color: Intense ruby red, with possible violet reflections.
- Aroma: Aromas of red fruits such as cherries and plums, often accompanied by spicy notes and sometimes floral hints.
- Flavor: On the palate, Gutturnio is distinguished by its lively acidity and well-integrated tannins. The taste is fruity, with some complexity and a persistent finish.
- Alcohol Content: Usually varies from 12% to 14.5%.
- Production Method: Gutturnio can be produced in both still (tranquillo) and sparkling versions. The sparkling version is often made through a natural second fermentation, giving the wine its characteristic effervescence.

Food Pairings:

With its combination of acidity and fruitiness, Gutturnio offers interesting food pairing possibilities:

- Meat Dishes: Ideal with red meats, such as roasts, steaks, and braised dishes. Its structure and acidity pair well with the rich and intense flavors of the meat.
- Emilian Cuisine: Pairs perfectly with traditional dishes of the region, such as stuffed pasta (tortelli piacentini
- and dishes based on mushrooms and truffles.
- Cured Meats and Cold Cuts: Excellent with the wide range of cured meats typical of Emilia-Romagna, such as coppa piacentina, pancetta, and salami.

- Cheeses: Classic pairing with medium-aged cheeses, such as Grana Padano and Provolone.
- Homestyle Cooking: Adapts well to robust homestyle dishes, such as stews and casseroles, thanks to its ability to balance richness and intense flavors.
- Mushroom-Based Dishes: The aroma and flavor of Gutturnio adapt well to mushroom-based dishes, such as risottos or mushroom sauces for pasta.
- Hearty Vegetarian Dishes: Also suitable for richer and more flavorful vegetarian dishes, such as eggplant parmigiana or legume-based dishes.
- Barbecue and Grilling: The sparkling version of Gutturnio is particularly suitable for accompanying mixed grills, barbecues, and flavorful dishes cooked on the grill.

Gutturnio is a wine that fully expresses the character of its land of origin, offering a range of food pairings that range from traditional dishes of Emilian-Romagnola cuisine to more creative and international choices. Its versatility makes it suitable for various occasions, capable of enhancing the flavors of the foods with which it is paired and providing an authentic and richly enjoyable gastronomic experience.

Technical Sheet: Cagnina di Romagna wine

Origin and Designation: Cagnina di Romagna is a traditional sweet red wine from Romagna, part of the Emilia-Romagna region in Italy. This wine has a long history in the region and is primarily produced in the coastal area.

- Grape Variety: Mainly made from Terrano grapes (locally known as Refosco).

Organoleptic Characteristics:

- Color: Vibrant ruby red, tending towards darker shades with aging.
- Aroma: Intense and fruity, with characteristic notes of fresh fruits like cherries and raspberries, and sometimes floral hints.
- Flavor: On the palate, Cagnina di Romagna is sweet, soft, and harmonious, with a pleasing balance between sweetness and acidity. The presence of fruit is evident, making it enjoyable and easy to drink.
- Alcohol Content: Generally around 10-12%.
- Production Method: Cagnina di Romagna is produced through a short fermentation process, which preserves the grape's natural sugars and part of its fruity character.

Food Pairings:

With its sweet and fruity profile, Cagnina di Romagna offers interesting and often surprising pairings:

- Sweets and Desserts: Pairs beautifully with baked desserts, especially those based on fruit, such as tarts and apple or cherry pies. Its sweetness and fruity notes harmonize well with the sweet flavors of desserts.
- Cheeses: Surprisingly, Cagnina di Romagna can be paired with cheeses, especially blue cheeses or soft

cheeses. The wine's sweetness balances the strong and spicy flavors of the cheeses.
- Asian Cuisine: An unconventional but intriguing pairing is with Asian dishes that feature some sweetness, such as certain sweet curries or meat dishes with sweet and sour sauces.
- Fresh and Dried Fruit: Perfect also as an accompaniment to a fresh fruit salad or dishes that include dried fruit, like figs.
- Light Meat Dishes: Can be paired with non-spicy or heavy meat dishes, such as roasts or light stews, where the wine's sweetness adds an interesting contrast.
- Light Appetizers: Works well with light appetizers, especially those that include sweet or fruity components.
- Aperitif: Thanks to its sweetness and lightness, Cagnina di Romagna can also be an excellent choice as an aperitif wine, especially in casual settings or gatherings.

In conclusion, Cagnina di Romagna is a wine that, with its sweetness and fruity character, offers a unique and pleasantly different tasting experience from traditional red wines. Its versatility in food pairings makes it an excellent choice for exploring original and surprising culinary combinations, making it a wine capable of satisfying a variety of palates and preferences.

Technical Sheet: Bianco di Custoza

Origin and Designation: Bianco di Custoza is a white wine primarily from the Lake Garda area in Veneto. Although this region is not part of Emilia-Romagna, the wine is sometimes also produced in the neighboring areas of the region.

- Grape Varieties: This wine is a blend of several grape varieties, which may include Trebbiano Toscano, Garganega, Tocai Friulano, Cortese, and Malvasia. This combination creates a unique and complex profile.

Organoleptic Characteristics:

- Color: Straw yellow, often with greenish reflections.
- Aroma: Delicate and fresh aroma, with floral notes and fruit such as apple, pear, and citrus, sometimes with hints of almond.
- Flavor: On the palate, it is light and refreshing, with good acidity and fruity notes that mirror the aromas. Some Bianco di Custoza may exhibit a slight minerality.
- Alcohol Content: Generally between 12% and 13%.
- Production Method: The vinification of Bianco di Custoza follows the traditional method for white wines, with fermentation at controlled temperatures to preserve the fresh and fruity aromas of the grape blend.

Food Pairings:

Thanks to its freshness and aromatic profile, Bianco di Custoza pairs well with a variety of foods:

- Appetizers and Snacks: Pairs well with light starters, such as fresh salads, fish carpaccio, and vegetable appetizers.
- Fish and Seafood Dishes: Its light and refreshing character makes it ideal for accompanying fish dishes, both grilled and stewed, and a variety of seafood.
- Asian Cuisine: Can be a good match with Asian dishes, particularly those not too spicy, like sushi and sashimi.
- Fresh and Light Cheeses: Excellent with fresh or soft cheeses, such as mozzarella or goat cheese.
- Vegetarian Dishes: Matches well with light vegetarian dishes, such as salads, grilled vegetables, and tofu-based dishes.
- Pasta and Risottos: Interesting pairings with light main courses, such as pasta with vegetables or seafood risottos.
- Poultry and White Meats: Can be paired with chicken or turkey dishes, especially if cooked with herbs or light dressings.

In conclusion, Bianco di Custoza is a versatile and enjoyable wine, capable of pairing with a wide range of dishes. Its lightness and freshness make it particularly suitable for summer occasions and outdoor meals, offering a refreshing and pleasant tasting experience.

Technical Sheet: Barbera dell'Emilia wine

Origin and Designation: Barbera dell'Emilia is a red wine produced in the Emilia-Romagna region of Italy. While Barbera is more commonly associated with Piedmont, the variety is also widely cultivated in Emilia, where it produces distinctive wines.

- Grape Variety: Primarily made from the Barbera grape variety, known for its lively acidity and fruity profiles.

Organoleptic Characteristics:

- Color: Intense ruby red, with possible violet hues.
- Aroma: Aromas of ripe red fruits like cherries an
- plums, often with earthy and spicy notes.
- Flavor: Characterized by marked acidity and red fruit flavors. Barbera dell'Emilia can range from light and fruity wines to more structured and complex versions, depending on the vinification method and possible aging in wood.
- Alcohol Content: Generally varies between 12% and 14%.
- Production Method: The vinification of Barbera dell'Emilia tends to emphasize freshness and fruit, with some producers using wood aging to add complexity and structure to the wine.

Food Pairings:

With its lively acidity and fruity profiles, Barbera dell'Emilia offers a wide range of pairing possibilities:

- **Meat Dishes:** The wine pairs well with a variety of meat dishes, including roasts, stews, and steaks, where the wine's acidity balances the richness of the meat.
- **Emilia-Romagna Cuisine:** Matches perfectly with typical dishes of the region, such as lasagna, Bolognese ragù, and dishes based on mushrooms and truffles.
- **Cured Meats and Cheeses:** Excellent with a broad range of cured meats and cheeses, especially those from the Emilia-Romagna tradition, like Prosciutto di Parma, Salame di Felino, and Parmigiano Reggiano.
- **Tomato-Based Dishes:** The acidity and freshness of Barbera dell'Emilia pair well with tomato-based dishes, such as pasta with tomato sauce and pizza.
- **Grilled Foods:** The wine is an excellent accompaniment for grilled foods, both meat and vegetables, thanks to its ability to balance smoked and grilled flavors.
- **Vegetarian Cuisine:** Interesting pairings can be found with hearty vegetarian dishes, such as eggplant parmigiana or legume-based dishes.
- **Spicy Foods:** In some variants, especially those slightly more robust, Barbera dell'Emilia can also be paired with mildly spicy foods, offering a good contrast of flavors.

In conclusion, Barbera dell'Emilia is an extremely versatile wine suitable for a wide range of dishes. Its characteristic acidity and fruity profiles make it ideal for accompanying a variety of flavors, from traditional Emilia-Romagna cuisine to international dishes, making it an excellent option for both everyday meals and special occasions.

HISTORIC WINERIES OF EMILIA-ROMAGNA

The historic wineries of Emilia-Romagna are much more than simple wine producers; they are true guardians of an invaluable cultural and historical heritage. These places have played a fundamental role in defining the wine identity of the region. Through generations, they have refined the art of viticulture and winemaking, preserving traditional techniques and indigenous grape varieties.

These ancient establishments do not just produce wines that reflect the authenticity of the territory but also serve as gateways to the living history of Emilia-Romagna. Visiting them is to embark on a journey through time, among ancient oak barrels, centuries-old cellars, and vineyards rich in history. The tastings offered allow visitors to directly explore the evolution of Emilia-Romagnolo wine.

A tour of Emilia-Romagna's historic wineries is a fascinating journey into the region's wine history. These facilities, some standing for centuries, are living testimonies that tell stories of families, traditions, and dedication to viticulture. Among the most renowned, here are some significant examples and their locations:

Antica Corte Pallavicina Winery: Located in Polesine Parmense, near Parma, this historic winery is famous not only for its wines but also for producing high-quality cured meats. The winery is part of a complex that includes an ancient castle and a farm.

Cleto Chiarli Winery: One of the oldest and most prestigious wineries in the region, located in Modena. Founded in 1860, Cleto Chiarli is known for producing high-quality Lambrusco and other local wines.

Tenuta Pederzana: Situated in Castelvetro di Modena, Tenuta Pederzana is another historic producer of Lambrusco. Its vineyards are in one of the most prestigious areas for the production of Lambrusco Grasparossa.

Venturini Baldini Winery: Located in the hills near Reggio Emilia, this winery is renowned for its Lambrusco and sparkling white wines. The estate includes an elegant 17th-century palace.

Albinea Canali Winery: Founded in 1934 in Reggio Emilia, it is known for its range of Lambrusco and other sparkling wines. The winery combines traditional methods with modern technology.

Casa Vinicola Zonin in Gambellara: While its main headquarters is in Veneto, Zonin also owns vineyards and produces wine in

Emilia-Romagna. It is one of the largest and most recognized wineries in Italy.

Umberto Cesari Winery: Located near Bologna, this winery is renowned for its red wines, particularly Sangiovese. The estate combines tradition with innovation, producing some of the region's finest wines.

Visit these historic wineries to immerse yourself in the wine culture of Emilia-Romagna, discovering how ancient traditions have been handed down and evolved over the centuries. Each winery offers a unique experience that connects visitors with the history, territory, and passion behind each bottle produced.

New Generations of Winemakers: Innovation and Sustainability

Alongside the historic wineries of Emilia-Romagna, we are witnessing the emergence of a new generation of winemakers, bringing freshness and innovation to the wine industry. These young producers, often educated in oenology and agronomy, are exploring new production methods, experimenting with non-traditional grape varieties, and adopting sustainable and organic practices.

Examples of Innovation and Sustainability:

Use of Organic and Biodynamic Techniques: Many of these new winemakers are adopting organic and biodynamic practices, reducing the use of pesticides and chemical fertilizers. For example, the "VerdeVite" winery uses biodynamic techniques to maintain the natural balance of the soil and promote biodiversity.

Renewable Energy and Carbon Footprint Reduction: Some wineries, like "SoleLuna," are investing in renewable energies, installing solar panels to reduce the carbon footprint of wine production and minimize environmental impact.

Reuse and Recycling: Initiatives such as water recycling and the reuse of winemaking by-products have become common practices. For instance, the "RiciclaVino" winery turns winemaking residues into compost to fertilize the vineyards.

Experimentation with Indigenous and Resistant Varieties: Interest in lesser-known and disease-resistant grape varieties is growing. The "UvaNativa" winery is working to rediscover and promote old Emilia-Romagnolo varieties, reducing the need for phytosanitary treatments.

Innovative Technologies in Production: The adoption of advanced technologies to monitor vineyards and optimize winemaking processes is another key aspect. "TechVino," for example, uses drones and sensors to monitor the health of the vines and optimize resource use.

This new wave of winemakers is contributing to renewed dynamism in the region's wine landscape. With an eye on quality and environmental impact, these producers are renewing the approach to viticulture, pushing the boundaries of tradition to create wines that are both a tribute to heritage and an expression of new ideas and techniques.

Through these practices, Emilia-Romagna is positioning itself as a leading region in wine innovation, demonstrating how tradition can coexist with innovation and sustainability, ensuring a prosperous and environmentally respectful future for the wine industry.

Synergy Between Tradition and Innovation

The beauty of the wine industry in Emilia-Romagna lies in its ability to harmonize tradition with innovation. While the historic wineries continue to be pillars of traditional winemaking, the new generations of winemakers are adding new nuances to the region's wine landscape.

This synergy between the old and the new is leading to a growing diversity in the region's wines. Consumers can now enjoy a wide range of wines, from classic Lambrusco and Sangiovese, made using traditional methods, to bold experiments with new varieties and sustainable techniques. This diversity not only enriches the region's wine offerings but also helps to strengthen its reputation internationally.

Emilia-Romagna is thus establishing itself as a region where respect for history blends with enthusiasm for the future. The historic wineries continue to be faithful custodians of traditions, while the new generations of winemakers bring a breath of fresh air and innovation. This balance between the past and present ensures that the region continues to be one of the most dynamic and interesting in the Italian wine landscape.

This beautiful region represents a unique territory in the world of wine, where history and innovation intertwine to create wines of exceptional quality and character. Its historic wineries and new generations of winemakers are working together to preserve the region's legacy, while exploring new possibilities and horizons, making Emilia-Romagna a must-visit destination for wine lovers and cultural enthusiasts.

FESTIVAL AND FAIRS OF EMILIA-ROMAGNA

Emilia-Romagna, a region renowned for its vibrant cultural liveliness and rich culinary tradition, hosts an annual calendar full of festivals and fairs that embody the pure joy of living. These events, held in picturesque villages, lively cities, and the green countryside, provide a unique opportunity to deeply immerse oneself in the local culture. They are occasions to savor culinary traditions, participate in historic rituals, and enjoy the genuine, warm hospitality of the region.

Each festival and fair in Emilia-Romagna is a unique experience that combines food, art, music, and traditions into a rich and diverse cultural tapestry. These events attract not only local residents but also visitors from around the world, eager to participate in these authentic celebrations. From centuries-old celebrations to modern festivals that highlight culinary and artistic innovations, the Emilia-Romagna festivity calendar is a mosaic of experiences.

During these celebrations, the streets and squares come alive with colors, sounds, and scents. Local chefs and artisan producers showcase their creations, offering tastings of traditional dishes and regional delights. The streets fill with music, from folk melodies to performances by modern bands, creating an electrifying atmosphere. Local artists and craftsmen display their talents, bringing the art and craft of the region to life through exhibitions and live demonstrations.

On these occasions, Emilia-Romagna reveals itself not just as a place of culinary indulgence but also as a melting pot of history and traditions. The festivals and fairs are deeply rooted in the historical and social heritage of the region, offering an authentic glimpse into the roots and evolution of the local culture. Participating in these events means not only enjoying a festive experience but also understanding and appreciating the history, stories, and way of life that define Emilia-Romagna.

The calendar of festivals and fairs in Emilia-Romagna is a journey through the vibrant heart of one of the most culturally rich regions in Italy. It offers moments of pure joy and celebration, where the community comes together to share their passion for their land, its traditions, and its culinary delights. At every event, there is a sense of belonging and regional pride, making Emilia-Romagna a must-visit destination for anyone wanting to experience the true essence of Italy.

The Porcino Mushroom Festival in Borgotaro

The Porcino Mushroom Festival in Borgotaro, celebrated every year in January, is an event dedicated to one of the most esteemed and renowned products of Emilia-Romagna: the porcino mushroom. This festival takes place in the picturesque town of Borgo Val di Taro, commonly known as Borgotaro, located in the province of Parma, in the heart of the Tuscan-Emilian Apennines.

Borgotaro, nestled in a landscape of rolling hills and lush valleys, is known not only for its natural beauty but also for the abundance of its PGI (Protected Geographical Indication) porcino mushrooms, which grow plentifully in the surrounding woods. The festival celebrates this precious gift of nature through a variety of activities and attractions.

During the Porcino Mushroom Festival, visitors have the opportunity to enjoy a wide range of dishes and local specialties made with porcino mushrooms. Restaurants and food stalls offer everything from classic tagliatelle with mushrooms to more innovative dishes that enhance the unique flavor of the porcino. It is also an opportunity to buy fresh mushrooms directly from local mushroom pickers, ensuring high-quality products.

Guided tours in the surrounding woods are a popular attraction of the festival. These walks allow participants to explore the natural habitat of the porcino mushrooms, learn to recognize them, and better understand their life cycle and environment. Led by local experts, these tours are an educational and enjoyable experience for nature and mushroom enthusiasts.

Furthermore, the festival includes cooking demonstrations where local and national chefs show how to prepare innovative and traditional dishes using porcino mushrooms. These demonstrations provide the audience with the chance to learn new recipes and culinary techniques.

In addition to culinary activities, the Porcino Mushroom Festival is also a time of cultural celebration, with live music, entertainment, and craft markets showcasing local craftsmanship. It is an opportunity for the Borgotaro community and visitors to share their passion for gastronomy, nature, and culture.

The Porcino Mushroom Festival in Borgotaro is not just a culinary event, but a complete cultural experience that celebrates one of the natural treasures of Emilia-Romagna, offering visitors an authentic taste of local life and the traditions of this fascinating Italian region.

The Carnival of Cento

The Carnival of Cento, celebrated in the town of Cento in Emilia-Romagna, is one of the most exuberant and colorful events in the region, known for its magnificent floats and intricately decorated masks. Inspired by the iconic Venice Carnival, this festival has earned an extraordinary reputation, attracting thousands of visitors each year.

This carnival is distinguished by its grand parades featuring huge allegorical floats. These floats are true masterpieces of engineering and art, designed and built by local artists and craftsmen. Each float is a mobile work of art, richly decorated and often animated with complex mechanisms that bring to life lively and dynamic scenes.

The masks, another highlight of the Cento Carnival, draw inspiration from both Venetian tradition and contemporary themes. Participants of all ages dress up in elaborate costumes and masks, creating an atmosphere of mystery and charm. These handmade masks represent not only a tribute to the tradition of Italian carnival but also an opportunity for creativity and imagination.

Beyond the parades of floats and masks, the Cento Carnival offers a wide range of activities and entertainment. Firework shows are a true spectacle, lighting up the sky with bright colors and intricate designs, while live concerts cater to all tastes, from traditional to modern genres, creating a festive and engaging atmosphere.

A unique aspect of the Cento Carnival is its community involvement. Schools, associations, and groups of citizens actively participate in creating and organizing the events, making the carnival a true community event that unites the town in a collective celebration of culture and tradition.

In conclusion, the Cento Carnival is much more than just a festival; it is a celebration of art, culture, and community. With its blend of tradition and creativity, this event offers a unique and unforgettable experience, reflecting the spirit and heart of Emilia-Romagna.

The Cento Carnival, in addition to its vibrant parades and masks, is also a must-visit for lovers of traditional Emilia-Romagna cuisine. During the carnival, the city transforms into a lively gastronomic hub, offering a wide range of culinary delights that celebrate the region's rich gastronomic heritage.

The streets and squares of Cento come alive with food stalls and markets where visitors can savor a variety of local dishes. These venues provide an opportunity to taste specialties such as tortellini, fried gnocchi, and cappelletti, accompanied by traditional cured meats like mortadella and prosciutto di Parma. Local cheeses like Parmigiano-Reggiano are also often offered in tastings alongside local jams and mustards.

A distinctive feature of the festival is also the presence of traditional sweets. Treats such as chiacchiere (or frappe), crostoli, and other fried delights are a constant presence, offering visitors a sweet taste of the carnival's culinary tradition. These sweets, often accompanied by a glass of local wine or coffee, are perfect for a delicious break between parades.

Moreover, during the Cento Carnival, many local restaurants and trattorias offer special menus, allowing visitors to immerse themselves in a more in-depth culinary experience. These menus often include typical dishes of Emilian-Romagna cuisine, prepared following traditional recipes and using high-quality local ingredients.

In summary, the Cento Carnival is an exceptional opportunity not only to admire art and culture but also to explore and savor the culinary riches of Emilia-Romagna. The combination of delicious food, festive atmosphere, and traditional culture makes this event a gastronomic and cultural experience not to be missed.

The Spring Festival in Modena

The Spring Festival in Modena, celebrated every March, is a lively event that marks the awakening of nature and the arrival of the spring season. This event is an ode to the fertility of the earth and the richness of the seasonal produce that spring brings. The festival not only celebrates the season with cultural events and entertainment but also serves as an important showcase for local cuisine.

Located in the heart of Emilia-Romagna, Modena is famous for its traditional cuisine and high-quality products. During the Spring Festival, the city streets and squares transform into a colorful open-air bazaar. Bustling markets offer a variety of fresh and local products, such as tender asparagus, juicy artichokes, and sweet, aromatic strawberries. These ingredients are the stars of the many stalls and food stands that populate the festival.

The festival is an opportunity for visitors to taste traditional Modenese dishes and culinary innovations. Local restaurants and trattorias offer special menus that highlight

the fresh and genuine flavors of spring. Dishes like asparagus risotto, grilled artichokes, and strawberry and walnut salads are just a few examples that visitors can enjoy, providing a gastronomic experience that is both authentically local and refreshingly seasonal.

In addition to savory dishes, local pastries play a significant role in the festival. Desserts made with fresh fruit, such as strawberry tarts and citrus cakes, delight the palates of visitors, offering a sweet end to the meals.

The Spring Festival is also a cultural event, with music and dance filling the streets. Local bands and street performers put on shows ranging from traditional folk music to more modern genres. Folk dances, often accompanied by traditional music, invite both locals and visitors to participate, creating an atmosphere of joyous community.

Furthermore, the festival hosts various events and activities for all ages, including cooking workshops, culinary demonstrations, and educational activities for children, which allow for learning more about local products and the culinary traditions of Modena.

The Spring Festival in Modena is an event that celebrates the richness and diversity of the cuisine and culture of Emilia-Romagna. Offering a mix of gastronomy, music, art, and tradition, this festival is an immersive experience that allows one to fully live the joy and abundance of spring in Italy.

Easter in Emilia-Romagna

Is a celebration rich in both religious and culinary traditions, marked by various events and festivities. Throughout the region, Easter symbolizes the rebirth and awakening of nature, which is also reflected in local eating habits.

Among the culinary traditions, a distinctive feature is the "pagnotta romagnola," an Easter bread with an ancient history, originating from the village of Sarsina. This bread-based pastry is consumed on Easter morning along with blessed eggs, salami, and Sangiovese wine. Its preparation requires a range of specific ingredients and a rather lengthy fermentation process.

The Easter lunch in Emilia-Romagna is characterized by the variety and richness of its dishes. Among the starters, lasagna is a classic, with the Bolognese recipe layering sheets of spinach pasta with ragù and béchamel sauce. Another typical first course is "tardura," a Romagna broth-based soup made with eggs, Parmesan, breadcrumbs, and nutmeg.

Lamb is the undisputed centerpiece of the main courses, prepared in various ways: stewed with fennel, roasted with peas, or in a Modenese version with balsamic vinegar. Rabbit is also a common feature on the Easter menu, usually prepared "alla cacciatora" or "in porchetta."

Easter desserts vary across the region. Among these, "Zuppa Inglese" is a classic from Reggio Emilia, a spoon dessert made of cream, chocolate, ladyfingers, and Alchermes liqueur. In Modena, the "Colomba di Pavullo" is cut, a unique version of the traditional Easter dove, with layers of leavened puff pastry filled with savor and served cold.

In addition to the Sarsina loaf, other traditional desserts include "panina pasquale," a rich cake with anise liqueur and cognac, orange and lemon peel, and the classic ciambella.

During Easter, Emilia-Romagna also hosts various gastronomic events, markets, and exhibitions, where visitors can taste and purchase local specialty products. Easter celebrations vary from province to province, with specific events in Bologna, Ferrara, Forlì-Cesena, Modena, Parma, Piacenza, Ravenna, Reggio nell'Emilia, and Rimini.

For more details on typical dishes and Easter traditions in Emilia-Romagna, you can visit websites such as emiliaromagnaturismo.it, travelemiliaromagna.it, and romagnaatavola.it.

During the Easter period, Emilia-Romagna hosts a variety of markets and processions that reflect the rich culture and traditions of the region. Although I have not found specific information on the Easter markets and processions for 2024, I can provide some general information based on similar events held in previous years.

Markets in Emilia-Romagna

The markets in Emilia-Romagna offer a wide range of items, including antiques, vintage items, crafts, and much more. Here are some examples of markets you might find:

In San Lazzaro di Savena (Bologna), there is an antiques market held on the first Sunday of the month.

In Pavullo (Modena), you can visit the Mercatino del Passato, also on the first weekend of the month.

In Bologna, the Mercato Antiquariato Città di Bologna takes place on the second Sunday of the month in Piazza Santo Stefano.

Other markets include events in Faenza, Stellata di Bondeno, and Gualtieri, among many others.

Religious Processions:

Religious processions during Easter are a significant aspect of the celebrations in Emilia-Romagna, although I do not have specific details on the 2024 processions. These events often include solemn moments and portrayals of the Passion of Christ, reflecting the deeply religious roots of the region. For more detailed and up-to-date information, I recommend checking local websites or church programs closer to Easter.

Other Easter Events:

In addition to markets and processions, Easter in Emilia-Romagna may include festivals, fairs, feasts, and excursions, offering a wide variety of activities to suit all tastes.

For more information and specific details on Easter events in Emilia-Romagna, I suggest visiting regional event websites or contacting local tourist offices as the holiday approaches.

The "May of Bologna"

Is an event that transforms the city into a hub of cultural and artistic activities. Although I have not been able to find specific information about the 2024 edition of this festival, I can tell you that similar events in Bologna include a wide range of activities such as art exhibitions, concerts, theatrical performances, and film festivals, taking place in various locations from historic squares to theaters. Bologna's calendar is rich with cultural events offering numerous opportunities to explore art, music, cinema, and much more.

For more specific details and updates on the 2024 edition of the "May of Bologna," I recommend keeping an eye on Bologna's official event and tourism sites such as Bologna Welcome.

The Tortellino Festival in Castelfranco Emilia

The Tortellino Festival in Castelfranco Emilia is an annual event that celebrates the famous typical dish of the region. The festival usually takes place in the second week of September, at the same time as the Feast of San Nico-la. During the festival, visitors have the opportunity to taste traditional handmade tortellini, prepared by local sfoglie masters. The typical recipe includes a filling of pork loin, Modena ham, Bologna mortadella, Parmigiano Reggiano, eggs, salt and nutmeg, all served in capon broth.

The Tortellino Festival also offers a variety of other activities and shows, including free concerts and events. A highlight is the historical procession that takes place along the Via Emilia, ending with a historical re-enactment that tells the legend of the birth of the tortellino.

For more information on the detailed program and the exact dates of the event, we recommend consulting the website of the La San Nicola Association, which organizes the event.

The Parma Ham Festival

The Parma Ham Festival is an annual event that celebrates the famous Parma Ham, recognized as one of the most prized cured meats in the world. The 2023 edition of the festival took place from September 1st to 3rd, and it can be assumed that the dates for 2024 will be similar. The festival takes place mainly in Langhirano, which is known as the "Cittadella del Pro-sciutto di Parma".

During the festival, visitors have the unique opportunity to discover how Parma Ham is produced through guided tours of ham factories in the ham production area. These visits, called "Open Windows", allow producers to illustrate the secrets of processing pork legs which, thanks to a magical combination of climate, tradition and passion, are transformed into Parma Ham. Reservation is required to participate in these visits.

In addition to guided tours, the festival offers a wide range of cultural and gastronomic events, including ham tastings and pairings with other fresh, simple foods. The festival is also an excellent opportunity to appreciate the cultural and natural beauty of the places of origin of Parma Ham.

For further information on the festival program and the proposed activities, we recommend consulting the official website of the Parma Ham Festival and following the updates for the 2024 edition.

The Palio of Ferrara

The Palio di Ferrara, which takes place in May, is one of the oldest equestrian competitions in Italy, with roots dating back to 1279. This historical and cultural event is characterized by a series of celebrations that culminate with the exciting horse races in Piazza Ariostea, traditionally on the last Saturday in May.

The Palio of Ferrara is not only an equestrian race, but also a dive into the Renaissance with costume parades, flag-waving competitions and open-air dinners. More than 1000 figures in Renaissance clothes participate in the Magnificent historical procession, recreating the atmosphere of the Este era. During the month of May, the city of Ferrara comes alive with various events which include ancient games of the Este flags and the blessing of the Palios, as well as the obligatory trials of horses and donkeys.

In addition to horse racing, there are competitions for boys (Corsa dei putti) and girls (Corsa delle putte), as well as the traditional donkey race. Each race is associated with a different colored Palio, representing the various districts of the city.

For further information on the specific program and related events, it is advisable to visit the official website of the Palio di

Ferrara. This event offers an extraordinary opportunity to experience the tradition and culture of Ferrara, as well as to enjoy the historical and artistic beauties of the city.

For more details, you can visit the Ferrara Terra e Acqua and Palio di Ferrara sites.

The grape harvest in Romagna

The grape harvest in Emilia-Romagna, which includes both the Emilian and Romagna sides, is a very important annual event for the region, given its renowned wine production. The harvest situation can vary considerably depending on the climatic conditions and the specific territory.

Regarding the 2023 edition of the grape harvest in Emilia-Romagna, it was observed that the different areas were affected by the effects of climate change. While in Emilia, despite the hailstorms, production showed some resistance, Romagna suffered a strong impact due to the floods. In particular, significant damage was reported in the Trebbiano and Sangiovese vineyards in the Ravenna and Forlì plains, as well as problems of torrential rain and landslides in the Romagna and Imola hills, affecting the Albana, Sangiovese and Chardonnay vineyards.

During the harvest period, several wineries and farms in the region organize special events, such as wine tastings and guided tours of the vineyards, to celebrate this important phase of the wine cycle. These activities offer visitors the opportunity to learn more about the wine production process and taste local products.

For more detailed information on specific events related to the grape harvest in Emilia-Romagna, you can refer to sites such as Eventiesa-gre.it, which provide a calendar of food and wine events in the region, including those related to the grape harvest.

The San Luca Fair in Bologna

The San Luca Fair in Bologna is one of the most anticipated and historic traditional events in the city. However, I was unable to find specific information about the 2024 edition of the San Luca Fair in the search results. Generally, this fair takes place in October and represents one of the oldest agricultural fairs in Italy, offering displays of local products, rides, and various forms of entertainment.

To obtain updated and detailed information on the 2024 edition, I recommend you regularly consult the sites dedicated to events in Bologna such as Bologna Welcome or the official BolognaFiere website. These sites offer a complete calendar of events in the city, including details on dates, times, and specific programs for each fair and event.

The Truffle Festival in Sant'Agata Feltria

The Sant'Agata Feltria White Truffle Fair is an annual event that celebrates the prized white truffle. Generally, this festival takes place on Sundays in October. During the event, visitors can immerse themselves in a suggestive and fragrant atmosphere, stroll through the streets and squares of the town, admiring the numerous typical products present.

The fair is also an opportunity to taste the local prized white truffle in traditional dishes offered in participating restaurants. In addition to truffle tasting, the event includes traveling shows, music, animations and exhibitions, making it a complete cultural and gastronomic experience.

Regarding the next edition, there is no certain information available yet. For specific updates and details on dates and programmes, we recommend consulting the website of the Pro-Loco of Sant'Agata Feltria or related pages. These sources provide useful and up-to-date information on upcoming events "The Christmas markets in Emilia-Romagna"

Christmas Markets

The Christmas markets in Emilia-Romagna offer a variety of festive and cultural experiences across different cities of the region. Here are some examples of markets taking place in Emilia-Romagna:

Bologna: The city hosts several Christmas markets, including the Christmas Fair in Via Altabella (from November 18, 2023, to January 8, 2024) and the Ancient Fair of Santa Lucia under the Portico dei Servi on Strada Maggiore (from November 10 to December 26, 2023).

Cervia: The Cervia Market is held from December 8, 2023, to January 7, 2024, offering a unique festive atmosphere.

Cesenatico: Cesenatico organizes its Christmas market on Anita Garibaldi Street from December 2, 2023, to January 7, 2024.

Ferrara: The Christmas Village of Ferrara takes place in Piazza Trento Trieste until January 7, 2024.

Ravenna: Ravenna hosts its traditional market in Piazza del Popolo from December 2, 2023, to January 7, 2024.

Rimini: In Rimini, the Christmas Market runs from November 25, 2023, to January 7, 2024.

Sant'Agata Feltria: The Christmas Village of Sant'Agata Feltria is held from December 3 to 17, 2023, in the historic center.

These markets offer a variety of gastronomic products, handicrafts, Christmas decorations, and many other gift ideas, creating a magical and festive atmosphere typical of the Christmas period. For more details and to discover other markets in the region, you can visit sites like Mercatini di Natale, Il Turista, and Mercatino di Natale.

Every month in Emilia-Romagna offers something unique and memorable, making this region a place where tradition blends with celebration, and where every visit promises an unforgettable experience.

FRESH AND LEAVENED DOUGH: THE ART OF MANUALITY

In the heart of Italy, where the hills meet the blue sky, lies Emilia-Romagna, a region famous for its rich culinary tradition. In this area, fresh pasta and leavened products are not simple dishes, but true symbols of an ancient art, handed down from generation to generation: the art of manual skill.

Fresh pasta, with its variety of shapes and fillings, is an emblem of this region. Tortellino, for example, is not just a dish, but a story of love and creativity. It is said that its shape is inspired by the navel of Venus, a tribute to divine beauty. Each fold of this delight contains not only tasty fillings, but also centuries of history and tradition.

Another pillar of Emilia-Romagna cuisine are leavened products, from fragrant bread and focaccia to soft piadine. The piadina, in particular, is a true symbol of conviviality. This simple disk of flour, water, lard and salt, cooked on hot stones or texts, transforms into a unifying element, a dish that brings families and friends together around the fire.

The secret of these products lies not only in the quality ingredients, but also in the manual skill of the artisans. Every gesture, from mixing the dough to its processing, is the result of years of experience and passion. In Emilia-Romagna, the preparation of dough and leavened products is considered an art, an almost sacred ritual that requires patience, precision and, above all, love for tradition.

But the art of manual skills in Emilia-Romagna is not just a legacy of the past. It lives and evolves, thanks to the commitment of chefs and artisans who, while respecting tradition, experiment with new flavors and techniques. Starred restaurants and small taverns offer unique culinary experiences, where fresh pasta and leavened products are the protagonists of innovative and surprising dishes.

Furthermore, the region witnesses numerous events and festivals dedicated to fresh pasta and leavened products, where experts and enthusiasts meet to celebrate this art. During these occasions, the streets of the cities and villages come alive, with hand-pastry demonstrations, tastings and workshops.

Fresh pasta and leavened products, in Emilia-Romagna, are much more than simple foods. They are expressions of a profound cultural heritage, a tangible link with the history and identity of this land. For those who visit this region, savoring a plate of fresh pasta or a bite of a soft piadina is not only a pleasure for the palate, but a real journey into the culture and tradition of a people who have made The art of manual skill is his priceless treasure.

THE SEA AND THE HILL: GASTRO-NOMIC DIVERSITYCA

Emilia-Romagna, an Italian region renowned for its extraordinary gastronomic diversity, extends from the green hills of the Apennines to the blue waters of the Adriatic. This land, where the sea meets the hill, offers a culinary panorama as varied as it is fascinating, testifying to how the territory profoundly influences culinary traditions.

On the coasts of Emilia-Romagna, the sea plays a fundamental role in the local diet. Here, seafood is not just ingredients, but the protagonists of dishes that tell stories of fishermen and ancient seafaring traditions. The mussels from Marina di Ravenna, the prawns from Cattolica, and the clams from the Po Delta are just some examples of the delights that can be tasted. The symbolic dish of the coast is "Brodetto", a fish soup that varies in ingredients and preparation from one port to another, reflecting the diversity of the communities that prepare it.

In contrast, the hilly hinterland offers a culinary panorama rooted in the land and agricultural tradition. Here, the products of the earth such as mushrooms, truffles, and a variety of vegetables and fruits are the protagonists. The cured meats and cheeses, such as Parma Ham and Parmigiano Reggiano, are expressions of ancient artisanal knowledge. The hills also offer fine wines, such as Lambrusco and Sangiovese, which perfectly accompany traditional dishes.

A unique aspect of Emilia-Romagna cuisine is the ability to blend these two worlds, marine and hilly, in unique and innovative dishes. An example is risotto, which can be prepared with seafood or land products, such as porcini mushrooms. This ability to combine different ingredients and flavors is testimony to the creativity and adaptability of the region's chefs.

The gastronomic diversity of Emilia-Romagna is also linked to its festivals and festivals. These occasions are an opportunity to celebrate local products and to experiment with traditional and innovative recipes. During these festivals, both along the coast and in the hills, you can discover dishes that not only delight the palate, but also tell the story and culture of this fascinating region.

Emilia-Romagna offers a unique culinary journey, where the sea and the hills meet in a union of flavors and traditions. Every visit to this region is an opportunity to discover how the diversity of the territory is transformed into a culinary art that delights and surprises, making Emilia-Romagna an essential destination for lovers of good food.

Tortellini, Tagliatelle and Others

Emilia-Romagna, a region in the heart of Italy, is famous worldwide for its rich culinary tradition, particularly its pasta dishes. Among these, tortellini and tagliatelle stand out as true symbols of local cuisine, accompanied by a vast range of other pasta specialities. This article explores the secrets and techniques behind the creation of these culinary delights.

Tortellini, little jewels of Emilian cuisine, are famous for their tasty filling and their unique shape, which requires precise technique and years of practice to master. Originating from the city of Bologna, these small knots of egg pasta enclose a mixed meat filling, often a mix of raw ham, mortadella, Parmigiano Reggiano, and nutmeg. Legend has it that their shape is inspired by the ship of the goddess Venus, making them not just a dish, but a piece of local history.

Tagliatelle, another pride of the region, are known for their simplicity and their perfect pairing with the classic Bolognese ragù. The unwritten rule is that the width of the tagliatelle is 8 mm, measured al dente. This detail, together with their consistency, is fundamental to best capture the flavor of the sauce.

Beyond tortellini and tagliatelle, Emilia-Romagna boasts a wide variety of handmade pastas, such as cappelletti, gnocchi, and lasagna. Each pasta has its history, its techniques and its secrets, often passed down from generation to generation within families.

One of the most fascinating aspects of pasta in Emilia-Romagna is its close relationship with local holidays and traditions. Tortellini, for example, are a classic on Christmas tables, often served in capon broth, while tagliatelle are a Sunday dish par excellence, celebrating the family reunion.

The preparation of pasta in Emilia-Romagna is considered an art, which requires not only technical skills, but also a deep knowledge of the ingredients. The quality of the wheat used for the flour, the freshness of the eggs, and the care in preparing the filling or sauce are all crucial elements that contribute to the success of the dish.

Technology has also found space in this tradition, with the modernization of some production phases. However, many artisans and chefs continue to favor the manual approach, convinced that perfection can only be achieved through direct contact with the pasta.

Furthermore, the region is home to numerous cooking schools and workshops, where visitors can learn the secrets of handmade pasta. These courses offer an immersive experience in the local culinary culture and represent a unique opportunity to understand the depth and passion that characterize Emilia-Romagna cuisine.

Pasta in Emilia-Romagna is not just food. It is a cultural element, a symbol of regional identity and a means of artistic expression. Through tortellini, tagliatelle and other varieties of pasta, family stories are told, centuries-old traditions are perpetuated and the simplicity and richness of Italian cuisine is celebrated. Each dish embodies not only exquisite flavours, but also the dedication, love and history of a region that has made pasta one of its greatest glories.

Visiting Emilia-Romagna and tasting its pasta specialties means immersing yourself in a world where culinary tradition is alive, celebrated and constantly reinvented. It is an experience that goes beyond taste, touching the heart and soul of a generous land full of passion.

FISH ADND SEAFOOD

Emilia-Romagna, known for its rich culinary traditions, offers a true gastronomic treasure along its coast: dishes based on fish and seafood. This region, with its extension along the Adriatic, boasts a variety of recipes that celebrate the gifts of the sea, combining ancient flavors with modern culinary techniques.

The coastal cuisine of Emilia-Romagna is characterized by a great variety of fish and seafood, used in recipes ranging from light first courses to more substantial second courses. The freshness of the ingredients is fundamental: freshly caught fish, local mussels and clams, prawns and squid are all essential for the success of these preparations.

A classic of the Emilia-Romagna coast is the "Zuppa di Pesce", a rich soup that combines different types of fish and shellfish in a tasty broth, often enriched with tomatoes and aromatic herbs. Another iconic dish is the "Fish Brodetto", typical of various coastal cities, which varies slightly in ingredients and preparation from one place to another.

Pasta is not forgotten: the "Tagliatelle ai Frutti di Mare" are an example of how the sea and the land meet in a dish. Here, fresh pasta blends with a variety of seafood, creating a rich and flavorful dish.

Another specialty is the "Mixed Grilled Fish", where fish and shellfish are grilled to perfection, enhancing their natural flavors with a touch of olive oil and lemon.

We cannot talk about the cuisine of the Emilia-Romagna coast without mentioning the ancient recipes of preserved fish, such as "Alici Marina-te", where the anchovies are marinated in vinegar or lemon, a testimony to the tradition of preserving fish.

In addition to these traditional recipes, the cuisine of the coast in Emilia-Romagna is constantly enriched by new creations, where local chefs experiment with contemporary ingredients and techniques, always maintaining a link with tradition and the territory.

In conclusion, the coast of Emilia-Romagna offers a unique gastronomic journey, where the flavors of the sea are celebrated in a myriad of traditional and innovative dishes.

To offer a taste of this extraordinary cuisine, here are some typical recipes:

Romagnolo fish broth

This fish stew is a classic, prepared with a variety of local fish, tomato, garlic, white wine and herbs.

Brodetto di Pesce Romagnolo is a traditional fish soup from the Emilia-Romagna coast, rich in flavors and colors of the sea. The recipe may vary slightly from one city to another, but here I present a classic version.

Ingredients:

- 1 kg of mixed fish (e.g. redfish, skate, gurnard, mallet)
- 300 g of shellfish (e.g. clams, mussels)
- 200 g of prawns or scampi
- 1 medium onion, finely chopped
- 2 cloves garlic, minced
- 400 g of peeled tomatoes or tomato puree
- 1 glass of dry white wineExtra virgin olive oil
- Salt and Pepper To Taste.
- 1 sprig of chopped parsley
- Toast or bruschetta to serve

Procedure:

1. Preparation of the fish: Clean the fish well, removing the scales, the innards and cutting the fins. The molluscs must be well cleaned and purged. The prawns or scampi must be peeled.
2. Prepare the sauté: In a large saucepan, heat the olive oil and fry the onion and garlic until translucent.
3. Add the fish: First add the fish that require longer cooking (e.g. redfish, skate) and after a few minutes add the other fish, molluscs and prawns/prawns.
4. Deglaze with wine: Pour in the white wine and let the alcohol evaporate.
5. Addition of tomato: Add the peeled tomatoes or tomato puree, salt and pepper. Cover and leave to cook over medium-low heat for approximately 20-30 minutes. It

is important not to mix too much to avoid breaking the fish.
6. Finish cooking: At the end of cooking, add salt and pepper if necessary and sprinkle with chopped parsley.
7. Serve: Serve the broth hot accompanied by toasted bread or bruschetta, ideal for absorbing the tasty fish broth.

Note:

The choice of fish is crucial: it is important to use a variety of good quality fresh fish.

Romagnolo Fish Brodetto is a dish that improves the next day, so it can be prepared in advance.

Traditionally, each fisherman had his own version of brodetto, so don't hesitate to customize the recipe according to personal tastes or the availability of local fish.

This recipe represents the culinary tradition of the Emilia-Romagna coast, combining the simplicity of the ingredients with the richness of marine flavours. Have a good meal

Italian Noodles baked in foil

The recipe for Italian noodles baked in foil with Seafood is a typical specialty of Italian cuisine, particularly of the coastal regions. This dish combines the delicacy of tagliolini with the richness of the flavors of seafood, all cooked in foil to enhance the aromas. Here is a classic version of the recipe:

Ingredients:

- 400 g of fresh tagliolini
- 200 g of mussels
- 200 g of clams
- 200 g of peeled prawns
- 200 g of squid cut into rings
- 2 cloves of garlic
- 1 sprig of chopped parsley
- 250 ml of tomato puree
- 100 ml of white wine
- Extra virgin olive oil
- Salt and Pepper To Taste.
- Baking paper for the foil

Procedure:

1. Preparation of seafood: Clean mussels and clams well. Place the mussels and clams in a pan with a little water, cover and cook until they open. Filter the cooking water and set aside.
2. Cooking seafood: In a pan, fry the garlic in olive oil. Add the squid and after a few minutes the prawns. Pour in the white wine and let it evaporate. Add the tomato puree, salt and pepper and cook for about 10 minutes.
3. Preparation of Italian noodles baked in foil: Cook the tagliolini in plenty of salted water until al dente, drain them and mix them with the seafood in the pan.
4. Preparing the parcel: Cut a large sheet of baking paper. Arrange the tagliolini with the seafood in the centre, sprinkle with the chopped parsley and a drizzle of oil. Close the parcel, sealing the edges well.
5. Baking in foil: Place the foil on a baking tray and bake in a preheated oven at 200°C for about 10 minutes.
6. Serving: Open the parcel directly on the serving plate to retain all the flavors and aromas.

Note:

It is important to use the freshest seafood to ensure the best flavour.

Cooking in foil is a method that allows you to keep all the aromas and juices inside, creating a dish rich in flavour.

This dish is perfect for a special dinner or to impress guests with an elegant but relatively simple dish to prepare.

The Italian noodles baked in foil with Seafood represent a perfect fusion between land and sea, a dish that celebrates the freshness of the ingredients with a surprising presentation. Enjoy your meal!

Cuttlefish with peas

A classic combination of Romagna cuisine, where cuttlefish are cooked slowly with fresh peas, onion and a touch of tomato.

The Cuttlefish with Peas recipe is a classic Italian dish, particularly popular in coastal regions. It is a delicious combination of the delicate flavor of cuttlefish and the sweetness of peas, all cooked in a tasty sauce. Here's how to prepare it:

Ingredients:

- 500 g of cuttlefish cleaned and cut into small pieces
- 300 g of fresh or frozen peas
- 1 medium onion, finely chopped
- 2 cloves garlic, minced
- 200 ml of tomato puree or peeled tomatoes
- 100 ml of white wine
- Extra virgin olive oil
- Salt and Pepper To Taste.
- A sprig of chopped parsley
- Water or light broth, if necessary

Procedure:

1. Preparation of the cuttlefish: If they are not already clean, clean the cuttlefish by removing the inside, the beak and the skin. Cut them into small pieces or strips.
2. Sauté: In a large skillet, sauté chopped onion and garlic in olive oil until translucent.
3. Adding the cuttlefish: Add the cuttlefish to the pan and saute for a few minutes until starting to turn opaque.
4. Deglaze with wine: Pour the white wine over the cuttlefish and let the alcohol evaporate.
5. Adding tomato and peas: Add the tomato puree or peeled tomatoes, peas, salt and pepper. If the mixture appears too thick, add a little water or broth.
6. Cooking: Cover and cook over medium-low heat for about 30 minutes, until the cuttlefish are tender and the peas are cooked. If necessary, add salt and pepper to taste.
7. Finish with parsley: At the end of cooking, sprinkle with chopped parsley.
8. Serving: Cuttlefish with peas can be served as a second course, accompanied by crusty bread or, for a more substantial meal, white rice or polenta.

Note:

It is important not to overcook the cuttlefish to avoid them becoming rubbery.

This dish can also be made with canned peas, but fresh or frozen peas offer a milder flavor and better texture.

For a richer variation, you can add a little cream towards the end of cooking.

Cuttlefish with Peas is a simple dish but rich in flavour, perfect for those who love the flavors of the sea with a touch of earthly sweetness. Enjoy your meal!

Sardoncini in Beccafico alla Romagnola

Sardoncini stuffed with a mixture of breadcrumbs, pine nuts, raisins and herbs, rolled up and baked or grilled.

The recipe for Sardoncini a Beccafico alla Romagnola is a variant of the traditional Sicilian dish "Sarde a Beccafico". In this Romagna version, the sardines are stuffed with an aromatic mixture and then baked or grilled. Here's how to prepare them:

Ingredients:

- 500 g of fresh sardines, cleaned and opened like a book
- 100 g of breadcrumb
- 30 g of pine nuts
- 30 g of raisins, soaked in warm water
- 1 clove garlic, finely chopped
- 1 sprig of parsley, chopped
- Grated zest of 1 lemon
- Salt and Pepper To Taste.
- Extra virgin olive oil
- Lemon slices to serve

Method:

1. Preparation of the filling: In a bowl, mix the breadcrumbs, pine nuts, squeezed raisins, garlic, parsley, lemon zest, salt and pepper. Add a drizzle of extra virgin olive oil to obtain a moist but not too sticky mixture.
2. Stuff the sardines: Open the sardines like a book and fill them with the prepared mixture, then roll them up on themselves, starting from the head.
3. Preparation for cooking: Place the stuffed sardines on a baking tray lined with baking paper. Drizzle with a drizzle of extra virgin olive oil.
4. Cooking: Cook in a preheated oven at 180°C for approximately 15-20 minutes, until the sardines are golden and crispy. You can also grill them for a more intense flavor.
5. Serve: Serve the Sardoncini a Beccafico alla Romagnola hot, accompanied by slices of lemon.

Note:

Make sure the sardines are very fresh for the best result.

The filling can be customized according to taste: for example, adding a little chilli pepper for a spicy touch.

This dish is excellent both as an appetizer and as a second course, and pairs perfectly with a glass of fresh white wine.

The Sardoncini a Beccafico alla Romagnola are an exquisite example of how Italian cuisine can vary and adapt based on the regions, always maintaining a high level of taste and quality. Enjoy your meal!

In conclusion, these recipes represent just a taste of the rich culinary tradition of the Emilia-Romagna coast, a heritage that continues to delight and surprise palates around the world.

TRUFFLES, MUSHROOM, MEAT AND GAME

Emilia-Romagna, a region that extends from the beating heart of Italy to its vibrant Adriatic coasts, preserves a unique and rich gastronomic heritage in its internal areas. In its hills, where nature generously offers its fruits, we find some of the finest products of Italian cuisine: truffles, mushrooms, meat and game. These ingredients, collected or raised in a natural and uncontaminated environment, are the basis of recipes that tell stories of land and tradition.

Truffles, in particular, are a true gem of the Emilia-Romagna hills. The White Truffle of Sant' Agostino and the Black Truffle of Fragno are treasures sought after all over the world for their inebriating scent and unmistakable taste. These jewels of the earth are used in many recipes, often simple, to enhance their unique flavour.

Mushrooms, especially porcini mushrooms, also play a fundamental role in the cuisine of the region. Harvesting these wild mushrooms is a community-uniting activity, and their rich, earthy flavors enrich a wide variety of dishes, from simple omelettes to more elaborate risottos and pasta sauces.

The meat and game of the Emilia-Romagna hills are equally renowned. These products, deriving from local farming and sustainable hunting, offer robust and authentic flavours. Wild boar, roe deer and pheasant are just some examples of game that find their place in rich and substantial recipes, often accompanied by sauces and condiments that enhance their taste.

In these internal areas, the cuisine is a fascinating fusion of simplicity and refinement, where every ingredient is made the most of. Traditional cooking methods, such as grilling and stewing, are very widespread and help create dishes with an intense and memorable flavour.

Finally, for those who wish to explore the rich culinary panorama of the Emilia-Romagna hills, here is a list of 5 typical recipes, which embody the spirit and flavor of this land:

Tagliatelle with Black Truffle

A dish that celebrates simplicity, where the flavor of black truffle goes perfectly with fresh pasta.

Tagliatelle with Black Truffle is a sophisticated and delicious dish, typical of Italian cuisine, especially appreciated in regions where truffles are abundant. Here is a classic recipe to prepare this dish:

Ingredients:

- 300 g of fresh tagliatelle
- 1 fresh black truffle
- 2 cloves of garlic
- 100 g of butter
- Salt and Pepper To Taste.

1. Grated Parmigiano Reggiano (optional)
2. Chopped fresh parsley (for garnish)

Procedure:

1. Preparation of the truffle: Clean the black truffle with a brush under running water, then dry it well. Slice it finely with a truffle slicer or grate it with a grater with fine holes.
2. Cooking the tagliatelle: Bring a pan of salted water to the boil and cook the tagliatelle until al dente. Drain them, keeping a little of the cooking water.
3. Prepare the dressing: In a skillet, melt the butter over medium heat. Add the crushed garlic cloves and brown them, then remove them.
4. Add the tagliatelle to the sauce: Add the drained tagliatelle to the pan with the melted butter. If the mixture is too dry, add a little of the tagliatelle cooking water.
5. Add the truffle: Remove the pan from the heat and add the sliced (or grated) truffle, stirring well to distribute evenly. Taste and adjust salt and pepper to taste.
6. Serve: Serve the tagliatelle immediately, garnished with fresh chopped parsley and, if desired, a sprinkling of Parmigiano Reggiano.

Note:

The quality of the truffle is crucial in this dish. Make sure to use a fresh, aromatic truffle.

Fresh noodles are preferable for this dish, as they better absorb the flavour of the truffle and butter.

This dish is best enjoyed immediately after preparation to fully appreciate the truffle's aroma.

Tagliatelle al Tartufo Nero is an exquisite example of how a few high-quality ingredients can create a dish rich in flavour and texture. Enjoy!

Risotto with Porcini mushrooms

A classic risotto where porcini mushrooms are the stars, enhanced by a good broth and Parmesan cheese.

Risotto ai Porcini is a classic Italian dish, prized for its rich, earthy flavour. Porcini mushrooms, with their intense aroma, are the prota-gonists of this dish. Here is a traditional recipe for preparing a delicious Risotto ai Porcini.

Ingredients:

- 300 g risotto rice (e.g. Arborio, Carnaroli)
- 400 g fresh porcini mushrooms or 50 g dried porcini mushrooms
- 1 medium onion, finely chopped
- 1 clove of garlic, chopped
- 1 litre vegetable or chicken stock, kept warm
- 150 ml dry white wine
- 50 g butter
- 100 g grated Parmesan cheese

- Extra virgin olive oil
- Salt and black pepper to taste
- Chopped fresh parsley (for garnish)

Procedure:

1. Preparation of the mushrooms: If using dried porcini, soak them in hot water for about 20 minutes, then drain and chop them. If fresh porcini are used, clean them with a damp cloth and cut them into pieces.
2. Sauté: In a large saucepan, heat the olive oil and half the butter. Add the chopped onion and garlic, sautéing until translucent.
3. Adding the mushrooms: Add the porcini mushrooms to the pan and cook until golden brown.
4. Toasting the rice: Add the rice and toast it for a couple of minutes, stirring to let it flavour the sauté.
5. Deglaze with wine: Pour in the white wine and allow the alcohol to evaporate, while continuing to stir.
6. Cooking the risotto: Start adding the hot stock, one ladleful at a time, waiting for the liquid to be absorbed by the rice before adding the next. Continue for about 15-18 minutes, until the rice is al dente.
7. Creaming: Remove the risotto from the heat, add the Parmesan cheese, the remaining butter, salt and pepper. Stir well to create a creamy consistency.
8. Serve: Serve the risotto hot, garnishing with chopped parsley.

Notes:

If dried mushrooms are used, the soaking water can be filtered and added to the stock for more flavour.

It is important to stir the risotto continuously during cooking to avoid sticking and to obtain the right creaminess.

Taste the risotto towards the end of cooking to adjust the salt and make sure the rice is cooked just right.

Risotto with Porcini mushrooms is a comforting and tasty dish, perfect for an autumn dinner or any occasion when a warm and cosy dish is desired. Enjoy!

Stewed wild boar

A robust wild boar stew, slowly cooked with red wine, herbs and a touch of tomato, which enhances its gamey flavour.

Stewed wild boar is a robust and tasty dish, typical of Italian cuisine, particularly in regions where wild boar hunting is a tradition. Boar meat, due to its richness and unique taste, lends itself very well to being cooked slowly in stews. Here's how to prepare this traditional dish.

Ingredients:

- 1 kg of wild boar meat, cut into pieces
- 2 medium onions, chopped
- 3 carrots, chopped
- 4 celery sticks, chopped

- 3 cloves garlic, minced
- 500ml robust red wine
- 400 g of peeled tomatoes or tomato puree
- 2 bay leaves
- Sprigs of rosemary and thyme
- Extra virgin olive oil
- Salt and black pepper to taste
- Meat broth or water, if necessary
- Flour, to coat the meat (optional)
- Preparation and Cooking Times:
- Preparation: 30 minutes (plus marinating time, if possible, which is approximately 12 hours)
- Cooking: About 2-3 hours
- Total Time: Approximately 2 hours 30 minutes to 3 hours 30 minutes, excluding sea-nature

Procedure:

1. Marinate the meat: If possible, marinate the wild boar meat in red wine with garlic, bay leaves and rosemary overnight. This step helps tenderize the meat and reduces its gamey flavor.
2. Sauté: In a large saucepan, heat the olive oil and sauté the chickens, carrots and celery until soft.
3. Preparing the meat: If you marinated the meat, drain and dry it. If desired, lightly flour the pieces of meat. This will help create a thicker sauce.
4. Brown the meat: Add the meat to the saucepan and brown until browned on all sides.

5. Deglaze with wine: If you used the marinade, add the marinade wine to the saucepan. Otherwise, use fresh red wine. Allow the alcohol to evaporate.
6. Adding tomatoes and herbs: Add the tomatoes, garlic, bay leaf, rosemary and thyme. Salt and pepper to taste.
7. Slow cooking: Cover the saucepan and leave to simmer for at least 2-3 hours, adding broth or water if the sauce reduces too much. The meat should be tender and the sauce thick.
8. Serve: Remove the aromatic herbs and serve the hot stewed wild boar, accompanied by polenta, mashed potatoes or rustic bread.

Note:

Marinating is not essential, but is recommended to improve the tenderness and flavor of the meat.

Long cooking is crucial to make the wild boar meat soft and tasty.

This dish is even tastier if prepared a day in advance and re-heated before serving.

Stewed Boar is a dish that stands out for its intense flavor and rich consistency, a true delight for meat lovers. It is a perfect dish for the colder months and for special occasions, where you can appreciate the depth of its flavour. Enjoy your meal!

Pappardelle with Hare

A traditional recipe combining fresh pasta with a rich hare sauce, slow-cooked to ensure a deep and harmonious flavour.

The recipe for Pappardelle alla Lepre is a classic Italian dish, particularly appreciated for its rich flavour and inviting texture. Here's how to prepare it:

Ingredients:

- 500g pappardelle
- 1 whole hare, cleaned and cut into pieces
- 1 onion, finely chopped
- 2 cloves of garlic, chopped
- 1 carrot, chopped
- 1 celery stalk, chopped
- 250ml red wine
- 500ml meat stock
- 2 tablespoons tomato paste
- extra virgin olive oil
- Salt and pepper to taste
- Rosemary, bay leaves and thyme
- Grated parmesan cheese (optional)

Preparation:

1. Preparation of the Hare: In a large saucepan, heat the oil and roast the pieces of hare on all sides. Remove them and set them aside.
2. Sauté: In the same saucepan, add onion, garlic, carrot and celery. Cook until soft.

3. Cooking the Hare: Put the hare back in the saucepan, add the red wine and let the alcohol evaporate. Add the tomato paste, herbs, salt and pepper. Cover with meat stock.
4. Stewing: Simmer for approx. 2-3 hours, or until the meat is tender and comes away easily from the bones.
5. Preparing the Pappardelle: Meanwhile, cook the pappardelle in plenty of salted water until al dente, drain and mix with the hare sauce.
6. Serve: Serve hot, with a sprinkling of grated Parmesan cheese if desired.

Time:

1. Preparation: About 30 minutes
2. Cooking: About 2-3 hours

The total time for preparing Pappardelle alla Lepre is therefore about 2 hours and 30 minutes to 3 hours and 30 minutes. This dish requires patience and care in slow cooking the hare, but the end result is a rich and tasty dish that well represents the Italian culinary tradition. Enjoy!

Roast Pheasant with Mushroom Sauce

An elegant dish where pheasant is roasted to perfection and served with a creamy mushroom sauce, perfect for a special dinner.

Roast Pheasant with Mushroom Sauce is a refined and delicious dish, ideal for special occasions. Here's how to prepare it:

Ingredients:

- 1 whole pheasant (approx. 1-1.5 kg)
- 300 g mixed mushrooms (porcini, champignon, etc.)
- 1 onion, chopped
- 2 cloves of garlic, chopped
- 1 glass of white wine
- 500 ml chicken stock
- 2 sprigs of rosemary
- 2 sprigs of thyme
- extra virgin olive oil
- Butter
- Salt and pepper to taste

Preparation:

1. Preparing the Pheasant: Clean the pheasant, tie it up with kitchen string to keep its shape while cooking and season with salt and pepper.
2. Browning: In a large frying pan, heat the oil and a little butter. Brown the pheasant on all sides until evenly browned.
3. Cooking the Pheasant: Transfer the pheasant to a baking dish, add rosemary, thyme and half a glass of white wine. Bake in a preheated oven at 180°C for about 60-70 minutes, basting occasionally with stock.
4. Preparation of the Mushroom Sauce: In a pan, sauté onion and garlic in a little oil and butter. Add the chopped mushrooms and cook them until tender. Add the remaining white wine and let it reduce. Finally, add

some of the stock and cook until a thick sauce is obtained.
  5. Finishing and serving: Once cooked, allow the pheasant to rest for a few minutes before cutting it into slices. Serve the pheasant slices accompanied by the mushroom sauce.

Preparation and cooking time

- Preparation: Approx. 30 minutes (cleaning and preparing the pheasant and mushrooms, browning)

Cooking:

- Pheasant in the oven: Approx. 60-70 minutes
- Mushroom Sauce: Approx. 20-30 minutes

The total time for preparing and cooking Roast Pheasant with Mushroom Sauce is therefore about 1 hour 50 minutes to 2 hours 10 minutes. This dish requires some care when cooking to ensure that the pheasant remains succulent and that the mushroom sauce has the desired consistency and flavour. Enjoy!

These dishes represent the richness and variety of the cuisine of the hills of Emilia-Romagna, a cuisine that draws with respect and wisdom from the gifts of nature, offering authentic and unforgettable gastronomic experiences.

SWEETS AND DESSERTS

Emilia-Romagna, with its rich culinary history, not only delights the palate with savoury dishes such as Parmigiano Reggiano and Balsamic Vinegar of Modena but is also the cradle of a varied and delicious dessert tradition. This northern Italian region is a true paradise for dessert lovers, offering a wide range of traditional desserts that tell stories of place, tradition and craftsmanship.

The sweetness of Emilia is characterised by authenticity and an abundance of sapors. From leavened cakes, perfect for festivities, to simpler desserts that can be enjoyed at any time of day, Emilia-Romagna offers a variety of sweets that satisfy every palate. Here are five of the region's most representative and popular recipes:

Sponge cake and custard

A classic of Emilian pastry making, Zuppa Inglese is a layered spoon dessert, made up of ladyfingers soaked in Alchermes and alternated with custard and chocolate cream. Its origin is disputed between Emilia and Tuscany, but it has become a symbol of Emilian sweetness, loved for its richness and the perfect balance between the different layers of flavour. Here's how to prepare it:

Ingredients:

- Ladyfingers (or Pavesini)
- 500 ml of custard
- 500 ml of chocolate cream
- Alkermes
- Cocoa powder for decorating
- For the Custard:
- 4 egg yolks
- 100 g of sugar
- 40 g of flour
- 500 ml of milk
- 1 vanilla pod
- For the Chocolate Cream:
- 500 ml of custard
- 150 g of dark chocolate

Preparation:

1. Custard: In a saucepan, mix the egg yolks with the sugar until the mixture is light and fluffy. Add the flour and mix well. Heat the milk with the vanilla, then pour it slowly over the egg mixture, stirring constantly. Cook

over a low heat, stirring until the cream thickens. Leave to cool.
2. Chocolate Cream: Melt the dark chocolate in a bain-marie or in the microwave. Mix it with 500 ml of cold custard.
3. Assembly: Quickly soak the ladyfingers in the Alchermes and place them on the bottom of a baking dish. Cover with a layer of custard, then with a layer of chocolate cream. Continue alternating layers until you run out of ingredients.
4. Refrigeration: Place the Zuppa Inglese in the refrigerator for at least 4 hours, preferably overnight.
5. Finishing: Before serving, dust the surface with cocoa powder.

Times:

1. Preparation: About 30 minutes (excluding the cooling time of the cream
2. Custard cooking: About 10 minutes
3. Refrigeration: At least 4 hours, ideally overnight
4. The total time for preparing the Zuppa Inglese, including refrigeration, is therefore approximately 4 hours and 40 minutes.

This dessert, rich and delicious, is perfect to conclude a special meal or to celebrate important occasions. The combination of creaminess and the light alcoholic note of Alchermes makes the Zuppa Inglese a unique pleasure for the palate. Enjoy your meal!

Barozzi cake

This black and dense cake, originally from Vignola, is a real hidden treasure. Made with almonds, coffee and cocoa, Barozzi Cake is flourless, making it naturally gluten-free. Its recipe is secret, but each homemade variation captures its essence: intense, rich and irresistibly chocolaty.

Ingredients:

- 200 g of sugar
- 150 g of soft butter
- 150 g finely chopped almonds
- 100 g of dark chocolate
- 3 eggs
- 1 tablespoon of instant coffee
- 1 tablespoon bitter cocoa powder
- 1 teaspoon baking powder

Preparation:

1. Preparation of the Compound: Melt the chocolate in a bain-marie or in the microwave and let it cool. In a bowl, cream the soft butter with the sugar until the mixture becomes frothy. Add the eggs one at a time, mixing well after each addition. Combine the melted chocolate, chopped almonds, instant coffee, cocoa and yeast. Mix until you obtain a homogeneous mixture.
2. Cooking: Pour the mixture into a buttered and floured cake mould. Bake in a preheated oven at 180°C for approximately 30-40 minutes. The cake is ready when a toothpick inserted into the center comes out clean.

3. Cooling: Leave the cake to cool in the mold for about 10 minutes, then turn it out and let it cool completely on a wire rack.
4. Finish: Once cold, the Barozzi Cake can be dusted with bitter cocoa powder or icing sugar, depending on your preferences.

Times:

1. Preparation: About 20 minutes
2. Cooking: 30-40 minutes
3. Cooling: At least 30 minutes

The total time for preparing the Barozzi cake is therefore approximately 1 hour and 30 minutes. This dessert, with a dense consistency and a rich and intensely chocolatey flavour, is perfect for accompanying a coffee or as an end to a meal on special occasions. Its main characteristic is the combination of the strong taste of chocolate with the aroma of coffee, which makes it a unique and appreciated dessert. Enjoy your meal!

Traditional Sweet cake from Romagna

The traditional Sweet cake from Romagna, also known as "Brazadela" or "Braza delo" in Romagna dialect, is a simple and genuine dessert, typical of the peasant tradition of Romagna. This donut has a slightly crunchy texture on the outside and soft on the inside, perfect for dipping in milk or wine. Here's how to prepare it:

Ingredients:

- 500 g of flour
- 200 g of sugar
- 100 g of soft butter
- 3 eggs
- 1 sachet of baking powder
- The grated zest of 1 lemon
- A pinch of salt
- Milk (if necessary)
- Powdered sugar to decorate (optional)

Preparation:

1. Dough: In a large bowl, mix the flour with the sugar, yeast and a pinch of salt. Add the soft butter cut into pieces, the eggs and the grated lemon zest. Knead until you obtain a homogeneous mixture. If the dough is too hard, add a little milk to soften it.
2. Form the Donut: On a lightly floured surface, work the dough until it forms a cylinder. Join the ends to create the classic donut shape.
3. Cooking: Place the donut on a baking tray lined with baking paper. Bake in a preheated oven at 180°C for around 30-40 minutes, or until golden brown
4. Cooling and Decorating: Allow the donut to cool before dusting it with icing sugar, if desired.

Times:

1. Preparation: About 20 minutes
2. Cooking: 30-40 minutes

The total time for preparing the traditional Sweet cake from Romagna is therefore approximately 50-60 minutes. This donut, with its simplicity and homemade taste, is perfect for a genuine and traditional breakfast or snack. The external crunchiness and internal softness make it irresistible, especially if accompanied by a cup of hot milk or, for the older ones, a glass of sweet wine. Enjoy your meal!

Bustreng

This dessert, typical of Romagna, is a cross between a cake and a pudding. Traditionally prepared in autumn and winter, Bustrengo is made with flour, stale bread, apples, dried figs and raisins. It is a simple dish but rich in flavours, perfect for warming up cold winter evenings.

Ingredients:

- 3 apples
- 100 g of raisins
- 100 g dried figs (optional)
- 200 g of flour
- 200 g of stale bread
- 100 g of sugar
- 500 ml of milk
- 3 eggs
- 1 sachet of baking powder
- Grated zest of 1 lemon
- 1 teaspoon ground cinnamon
- Extra virgin olive oil or butter for greasing

Preparation:

1. Preparation of the Ingredients: Soak the raisins in hot water. Cut the apples into small pieces and the dried figs, if used. Reduce the stale bread into crumbs.
2. Dough: In a large bowl, mix the flour with the bread, apples, raisins, figs, sugar, lemon zest and cinnamon. Add the eggs and milk, mixing until you obtain a smooth mixture. Add the yeast.
3. Cooking: Pour the mixture into a pan previously greased with oil or butter. Bake in a preheated oven at 180°C for about 60 minutes, until the surface becomes golden and crispy.
4. Cooling: Allow the Bustrengo to cool before cutting and serving it.

Times:

1. Preparation: About 30 minutes
2. Cooking: 60 minutes
3. Cooling: At least 30 minutes

The total time for preparing Bustreng is therefore approximately 2 hours. This rustic and comforting dessert is a real delight, with its moist and rich texture, enriched by the sweet notes of apples, raisins and figs. It is a dish that is linked to the Romagna peasant tradition, perfect for finishing a family meal or for a substantial snack on winter days. Enjoy your meal!

Spongata of Brescello

Spongata di Brescello is a typical dessert from Emilia-Romagna, in particular from the small municipality of Brescello. It is a kind of tart with a rich filling of jam, dried fruit, and spices. Traditionally, it is prepared during the Christmas period. Here is a recipe to make it:

Ingredients:

For the Shortcrust Pastry:

- 500 g of flour
- 200 g of sugar
- 200 g of butter
- 2 eggs
- 1 lemon (grated zest)

For the stuffing:

- 300 g of apricot jam
- 150 g of honey
- 100 g of chopped almonds
- 100g chopped walnuts
- 50 g of pine nuts
- 50 g of raisins
- 1 teaspoon ground cinnamon
- Grated zest of 1 lemon
- Grated zest of 1 orange

Preparation:

1. Preparation of the shortcrust pastry: Mix the flour with the sugar, add the butter cut into pieces, the eggs and the grated lemon zest. Knead until you obtain a homogeneous mixture. Leave to rest in the fridge for about 30 minutes.
2. Preparation of the Filling: In a bowl, mix the apricot jam with the honey, almonds, walnuts, pine nuts, raisins, cinnamon, and grated lemon and orange peel.
3. Assembly: Roll out two thirds of the shortcrust pastry and line the bottom and sides of a buttered and floured baking tray. Pour the filling over the pasta. Roll out the remaining dough and cover the filling.
4. Cooking: Bake in a preheated oven at 180°C for approximately 40-45 minutes, until the shortcrust pastry becomes golden.
5. Cooling: Allow the Spongata di Brescello to cool before cutting and serving it.

Times:

1. Shortcrust pastry preparation: About 15 minutes (plus 30 minutes of rest)
2. Filling preparation: About 15 minutes
3. Assembly: About 10 minutes
4. Cooking: 40-45 minutes
5. Cooling: At least 30 minutes

The total time for preparing the Spongata di Brescello is therefore approximately 2 hours and 20 minutes. This rich and aromatic dessert is perfect for the Christmas holidays or as a special dessert on festive occasions. The combination of dried fruit, jam and spices creates a mix of flavors that evokes the tradition and warmth of family gatherings. Enjoy your meal!

These sweets represent only a small part of the rich confectionery tradition of Emilia-Romagna, a region that knows how to seduce its guests with the delights of the palate. Each cake has a story to tell, linked to local traditions, festivities and moments of conviviality.

It is not uncommon to find these sweets in the pastry shops of Emilia, whose flavours and aromas evoke memories and traditions. Whether a sophisticated dessert like Zuppa Inglese or a rustic cake like Bustren-go, each dessert is an invitation to explore the culture and traditions of this magnificent Italian region.

Emilia-Romagna, then, is not only the land of bollito misto and lasagne, but also a place where sweetness is declined in a thousand ways, each with its own particular charm. From the simple pleasure of a Borlengo with Nutella to the complexity of a Torta Barozzi, there is always an Emilian dessert ready to delight and surprise.

THE IMPORTANCE OF PRESERVING CULINARY TRADITIONS

As we near the conclusion of our culinary journey through "A Tavola in Emilia-Romagna", it is essential to reflect on the vital importance of preserving culinary traditions in this region. Emilia-Romagna is not only a land of intense flavors and rich dishes, but it is also a proud guardian of a gastronomic culture that is passed down from generation to generation.

The culinary traditions of this region, ranging from homemade recipes to artisanal preparation techniques, constitute an intangible heritage that tells stories of communities, families and regional history. Each dish, from a simple Spongata di Brescello to a rich dish of Lasagne alla Bolognese, embodies centuries of knowledge, adaptations and passion.

The preservation of these traditions is not only a tribute to the past, but also a commitment to the future. In an era where globalization tends to standardize tastes and eating habits, keeping traditional recipes alive is a way to educate new generations about the value of cultural diversity and sustainability.

Furthermore, Emilia-Romagna cuisine is a shining example of how food can be a bridge between different cultures. The recipes we have explored in this book are not just instructions on how to prepare a dish, but are also invitations to sit at a communal table, share stories, and build relationships.

By concluding this book, we hope that readers have not only acquired a new repertoire of recipes to experiment with, but that they have also developed a deeper appreciation for the gastronomic culture of Emilia-Romagna. These recipes are more than just lists of ingredients and procedures; they are a journey through time and history, a celebration of flavors that have resisted the passing of time and fashion.

Emilia-Romagna cuisine teaches us the importance of food not only as nourishment, but as an expression of identity, as an art that tells of fertile lands, skilled hands, and passionate hearts. Through typical dishes, from the most elaborate to the simplest, the memory of a territory is passed down and a tangible connection with roots and traditions is built.

In a rapidly changing world, where the new often supplants the old, the preservation of culinary traditions is an act of resistance and love. It is an invitation to slow down, to reflect on the origins of what we eat, and to recognize the value of the work and dedication behind every dish.

As we close the pages of "A Tavola in Emilia-Romagna", we leave it to our readers to keep these traditions alive. We hope that every recipe tried and shared is a small step towards safeguarding a priceless culinary heritage, a heritage that we can proudly call ours. Have a safe journey through flavours, and may your table always be full of joy, sharing and tradition.

Printed in Great Britain
by Amazon